MW01123726

WERE NOT OUR
HEARTS BURNING!

Beth,

God bless you!
May the peace of Christ
be with you always

John Baker

WERE NOT OUR HEARTS BURNING!

REFLECTIONS ON GOD'S WORD FOR EVERYDAY LIVING

JOHN PALMER

A Division of WINEPRESS PUBLISHING

© 2006 by John Palmer. All rights reserved.

Pleasant Word (a division of WinePress Publishing, PO Box 428, Enumclaw, WA 98022) functions only as book publisher. As such, the ultimate design, content, editorial accuracy, and views expressed or implied in this work are those of the author.

No part of this publication may be reproduced, stored in a retrieval system or transmitted in any way by any means—electronic, mechanical, photocopy, recording or otherwise—without the prior permission of the copyright holder, except as provided by USA copyright law.

Unless otherwise noted, Scripture quotations in this book are taken from the New American Bible, copyright 1969, 1970, 1986, 1991 by the Confraternity of Christian Doctrine, Washington D.C.

ISBN 1-4141-0515-0
Library of Congress Catalog Card Number: 2005905606

To Doris and Jack Palmer, my mom and dad, who continue, by the example of their lives, to model God's love for me.

TABLE OF CONTENTS

FOREWORD

This is the day the Lord has made; let us rejoice in it and be glad.

(Psalms 118:24)

In early 2001 in an effort to enter into a deeper prayer life, I began writing a scriptural reflection each day based on the daily liturgical readings. At the urging of a few friends I began to share these reflections through e-mail, and found that between family and friends, I was sending the reflections to about twenty people each day. Soon others asked to be added to the e-mail list, and still others began to forward the reflections to their own family and friends. By the grace of God this ministry grew, until today more than 2,000 people worldwide are receiving and sharing God's Word in these reflections.

Through this ministry I have been truly blessed. God has changed my life. He has given me a new hunger for his holy Word in Scripture, and I continue to experience healing in both body and soul through the power of his Word. He has brought wonderful and holy people into my life, who continue to inspire and encourage my own spiritual growth.

By the grace of God and the anointing of the Holy Spirit, many others have been similarly blessed. I receive e-mail from people every day attesting to the power and the love of our God, and the powerful effect of his most holy Word in their lives. I hear from others who would like

Were Not Our Hearts Burning!

to share in this ministry but do not have computers, and still others who have expressed the desire to have a resource of targeted reflections for their study and prayer.

The writing of this book born of these ideas will hopefully be a blessing to all who are interested in coming closer to the Lord by experiencing the power of his Word in Holy Scripture. The reflections in this book are some of those that have been sent out as part of my daily ministry over the last three years.

Our Lord invites each one of us into the bright light of his love and grace. He invites each one of us to experience his love, grace, and goodness in our lives. Our God is so good, and he shares that goodness with us in the power of his Word in Scripture.

Praise be to God!

That at the name of Jesus every knee should bend, of those in heaven and on earth and under the earth, and every tongue confess that Jesus Christ is Lord, to the glory of God the Father.

(Philippians 2:10-11)

ACKNOWLEDGMENTS

I'm so blessed to have so many people who have supported and encouraged me as I worked on this project. Without the help of many people this book would not have become a reality.

First, I'd like to thank all of the people who have supported my "Reflections" ministry on the Internet. Your encouragement has been invaluable, as we have all experienced God in new ways through his Word in Scripture.

Second, thank you to my faith community of St. Columba in San Diego, and especially to the Charismatic Prayer Community, who continue to support and pray for me.

Finally, a big thank you to my family, especially to my wife, Phyllis, for all of her support; to my sister Susan Brauer, whose ideas and encouragement have kept me focused on this project; to my sister Lori Palmer, who had the unenviable task of proofreading and editing; and to my sister and brother-in-law, Chris and Bill Kneeland, who continue to support and work with me in this ministry.

INTRODUCTION

One of my favorite resurrection stories in Scripture is the appearance of Jesus to the two disciples on the road to Emmaus. (Luke 24:13-35) The two disciples' hearts were broken. They were lost. Then Jesus appeared to them. He interpreted for them all of the Scriptures that had referred to Jesus as Messiah. He revived their hope. He built their faith. And then he revealed himself to them in the breaking of the bread.

Many times in our own lives our hearts are broken. We are lost. We need the love and strength of Jesus in our lives. We need to have our hope revived and our faith built up. We need the powerful presence of the Lord in our lives. Our God offers this and more through the power of his Word in Scripture. Just as he explained the Scripture to the two disciples, he will give us knowledge of Scripture through the power of the Holy Spirit as we reflect on his Word and open our minds and hearts to his wisdom.

This book was written to help us open our lives to God's Word in Scripture. The readings and reflections in this book may be a good opportunity to begin to explore the Word of God, and its meaning for our lives. I have arranged the reflections according to themes, so that they may be used for study as the Lord leads us. Each reflection contains a Scripture site, as well as the reflection itself. I suggest that one way to use this book is as a daily help in prayer and study by reading the entire Scripture passage, and then by using the reflection as a way to commune with the Lord in prayer, letting him teach and bless our lives through his Word. This is just one suggestion, however individuals are encouraged to embrace these reflections in the way that is most meaningful for them. However you proceed, I know that as we open our hearts to God's Word in our lives, we will be able to say, as did the two disciples, "Were not our hearts burning (within us) while he spoke to us on the way, and opened the Scriptures to us?" (Luke 24:32)

1

In His Image

Everything for us starts with God's love. In his love we are created in his image. In his love we have our life. In his love we have our well-being and our joy. In his love we are forgiven. In his love we are sustained.

Prayer

Loving Father, as we contemplate your great love for us, help us experience your love more fully. Help us live in your love more completely. Help us celebrate our dignity and worth, born out of your tremendous love for us.

Were Not Our Hearts Burning!

(Genesis 1:1-31)

"God created man in his image, in the divine image he created him;
male and female he created them."

In this passage from Genesis the story of the creation of the world is told. We see the power and majesty of our God. We see his love for all that he has created. We see the care he takes in creating the world for the benefit of all of his creation. We see the delight he takes in the work of his hands. Everything on earth has been created with loving care by our most gracious God. He has given us dominion over all that he has created. We have been created by God in his image to master and have dominion over the earth. The Lord tells us with that dominion comes responsibility. He calls on us to see the love that he shows in creating all things. He calls us to see the beauty in ourselves and in our world through his caring, loving eyes. The Lord created all with a sense of balance. Everything he created has a purpose. Everything he created respects the beauty of life. We are called to respect the dignity of all the life God creates. It is in looking at our world through the wonder of our Creator that we see his majesty and glory. We see the love God has for each of us. In looking at creation through the glory of the Lord, we are given the love, strength, and grace to properly care for ourselves and all that God has given us.

In His Image

(Luke 15:11-32)

"While he was still a long way off, his father caught sight of him,
and was filled with compassion."

The story of the lost son is one of the most powerful stories demonstrating God's love for all of us. We cannot read and study this story without realizing that our God is a loving and forgiving Father. The story is filled with images of a father who is caring, understanding, compassionate, and loving to his child. Jesus tells us that our Father in heaven loves each one of us in the same way. Just as the father in the story gives his son his full inheritance unconditionally, so our Father has given us our inheritance. Many times in our lives we squander that inheritance. Through sinfulness, we turn our backs on our Father. We want to go it alone, and think that we do not need our Father. It is such a comfort for us to know that God is constantly waiting for us to return to him. Not only does he wait for us, but he actually looks for us to return. And when we do return to him, he is filled with joy to welcome us back and to restore us to full life in himself. Truly our God is a wonderful and loving Father. Let us pray that we always realize the power of God's love in our lives. Let us pray for the grace to always live in the love of the Lord, striving to return to him the tremendous love he constantly shows us.

Were Not Our Hearts Burning!

(Hosea 11:1-9)

"Yet it was I who taught Ephraim to walk, who took them in my
arms; I drew them with human cords, with bands of love; I fostered
them like one who raises an infant to his cheeks; yet, though I
stooped to feed my child, they did not know that I was their healer."

Our Lord's love for us is boundless. He loves us more than we can comprehend. He loves us with a love that cannot be shaken. Our Lord speaks
to us so beautifully through the prophet Hosea. He tells us of his love
and tenderness for each of us. He longs for us to know of his love, and
to accept his love in our lives. He tells us that it is when we experience
his love in our lives that we will be made whole. We will begin to be
healed of the pain and hurt in our lives. Let us pray that the Lord will
wrap our weak and hurting hearts in his most sacred heart, that we may
come to know his love and mercy in our lives. Let us turn over to the
care and tenderness of his most sacred heart the fear, pain, and sorrow
in our lives. Let us see in the Lord, in his love for us, as our healer. Let
us come to experience the boundless love of our Lord and Savior.

In His Image

(2 Corinthians 5:20-6:2)

"Working together, then, we appeal to you not to receive the grace of God in vain."

God loves us unconditionally. He showers his graces upon all of his children. He loves us so much that he has given us his only Son for our salvation. He gives us his might and power through the gift of the Holy Spirit, who teaches and guides us. All this and more he has given because we are his beloved children. He has created us, and his love and mercy for us are boundless. His grace is never ending. He desires that his grace have effect in us. He desires that the power and might he gives us through the Holy Spirit will keep us strong, living always in his light. He desires that we know him as our loving Father. Our Lord tells us that now is a good time for us to contemplate all that the Lord has given, and continues to give us, making sure that we are putting to good use all that the Lord gives for our benefit. It is a good time to examine our relationship with God as Father. It is a good time to make right the wrongs that we have committed, and to come to live once more in the bright light of God's goodness. Our God is calling us closer to himself. Let us listen and answer his call.

Were Not Our Hearts Burning!

(Isaiah 49:8-15)

"I will cut a road through all my mountains, and make my
highways level."

As we travel through this life of peaks and valleys, as we journey along
the ways which we ourselves make so difficult through our stubbornness
and sinfulness, our Lord wants us to know that he loves and cares for us
wherever we may be in our lives. Through the prophet Isaiah, the Lord
reminds us that his love for us is as pure and strong as a mother for her
infant. He tells us that he desires to make our paths straight. He longs
to make our journey through this life safer for us. Our Lord reminds us
that if we surrender ourselves to him, he will certainly help and protect
us. He tells us that if we follow his way, instead of trying to find our
own way, he will go before us to make level and straighten our path. If
we leave our care in his hands, our God tells us that our path will be
smoother. We will walk in his light, experiencing more peace, as we will
not be alone, but will be walking with him. Let us pray for the courage
to surrender our lives to the Lord. Let us give up our stubborn ways and
rely on the Lord for our help and protection. Let us rely on the beautiful
promises of the Lord, which we read in this passage from Isaiah. Let us
live in the strong and pure love that God has for each of us.

In His Image

(John 17:20-26)

"Father, they are your gift to me. I wish that where I am they also
may be with me, that they may see my glory that you gave me,
because you loved me before the foundation of the world."

How blessed we are to have Jesus as our Brother, our Friend, and our Redeemer. How blessed we are to know that Jesus would pray for us to the Father, as he does in this passage from John's Gospel, to know that we are felt by Jesus to be his gift from the Father. How blessed we are to know that Jesus considers each of us so precious that his desire for us is to be one with him and with our Father. The overwhelming gift of Jesus' love for us is evident in the words that he speaks on our behalf. As we read the prayer of Jesus for us, we cannot help but feel the great love that he has for us. We cannot help but feel the desire of Jesus that we be with him always. We cannot help but realize that even now Jesus is at the right hand of the Father interceding for each of us. Let us always be aware of Jesus' love for us. Let us strive to live our lives in the knowledge that we are blessed by the grace of Jesus, in the dignity that we have in him who loves each of us so much and considers each of us his most precious gift.

Were Not Our Hearts Burning!

(Luke 14:1-6)

"Then he said to them, 'Who among you, if your son or ox falls into a cistern, would not immediately pull him out on the sabbath day.'"

When Jesus walked on this earth he taught that the law was important. He told us that he had not come to abolish the law. He had come to fulfill the law. Jesus reminds us, however, that the law revolves around love. He reminds us that as Christian people we are called to put on the love of Christ in all that we do. We are called to follow the law in love. Jesus admonished the Jewish leaders, who many times put the law above love. The law, and not the spirit of the law, was most important to them. When we put on the love of Christ, we will be more able to follow his way for us. In love we will be better able to understand the path on which the Lord leads us. We will be better able to serve him in our lives. Let us pray that we always put on the love of Christ in our lives. Let us pray that we are able to more closely follow the example of Jesus, whose love and compassion give us hope and strength.

In His Image

(John 20:11-18)

"Jesus said to her, 'Mary!' She turned and said to him in Hebrew,
'Rabboni,' which means teacher."

Jesus knows us even better than we know ourselves. He is our Creator. He formed us. He loves us with an everlasting and unconditional love. Our souls long for our Lord. They long to touch him and live in his love and light. With the many concerns that we are faced with in our lives, we sometimes lose our focus on the Lord. In our sinfulness our souls are stifled, and we fail to see and recognize the Lord in the many ways in which he is present to us. In this passage, Mary, in her sorrow and grief, failed to recognize Jesus when he appeared to her. Earthly concerns kept her from recognizing him. It was when Jesus spoke her name with love and tenderness that her soul recognized her Creator. Her earthly concerns faded away, and Mary was again in the presence of her Lord. The Lord continues to call each of us by name. He continues to be present to us in our lives. He longs for the times when our souls recognize him and our earthly concerns melt away. He longs for us to always live in his love and his light.

Were Not Our Hearts Burning!

(Isaiah 42:1-7)

"Here is my servant whom I uphold, my chosen one with whom I am pleased, upon whom I have put my spirit; he shall bring forth justice to the nations, not crying out, not shouting, not making his voice heard in the street."

Jesus is our mighty and powerful Savior. He is all glorious. Yet he came into the world as one of us. He came into the world, the son of poor working-class people. He lived his whole life in a small area of the world, in the context of his upbringing and station in life. Yet, he has touched lives in all the world. Jesus chose to change the hearts and minds of people by his love rather than his power. He chose to bring people to the Father through his compassion and mercy. He lived in the power of the Holy Spirit and in the true faith that God was always with him. He lived a holy life, showing by example the way to please and glorify our Father in heaven. We are called to that same life of love and holiness. It can be a difficult life, because our society places so much emphasis on might and power. We are taught to fight for what we want. We are taught might is right. And yet we see that is not the Lord's way. His way is love and forgiveness, peace and mercy. Let us follow the example of Jesus. Let us be changed by his love and mercy. Then let us share what we have received with our families and friends. It is the love and grace of Jesus that will change our lives and our world. Praise be to God!

In His Image

(1 John 4:7-10)

"In this is love: not that we have loved God, but that he loved us and sent his Son as expiation for our sins."

St. John explains to us that we know love only because we are loved by our God. All love flows from God. We can only love God because he first loved us. St. John goes on to explain that it is the love of God that is our strength and our life. We see around us so much hate and distrust. We see so much anger and fear. We may even have anger or fear in our own lives. We can only begin to conquer those emotions by realizing and understanding the love God has for us. We can only begin to conquer those emotions by proclaiming and modeling the love that we receive from the Lord to the world around us. God is all about love. He is all about goodness. He longs for all of us to accept his love in our lives. He longs for all of us to know the depth of his love for us. Let us open our hearts to the love of God. Let us pray for the grace to understand the depth of God's love for us, as we listen to his Word in Scripture, as we listen to the words of Jesus, who shows us the face of God, and as we open our lives to the guidance of the Holy Spirit, who is the embodiment of the love of God and Jesus. Finally, let us strive to proclaim and model the love of God to those around us, and to the world that is in so much need of the experience of God's love.

Were Not Our Hearts Burning!

(Isaiah 40:1-11)

"Speak tenderly to Jerusalem, and proclaim to her that her service is at an end, her guilt is expiated; indeed she has received from the hand of the Lord double for all her sins."

Our God is kind and merciful. He wants only what is good for us. He longs for us to turn to him so that he may shower upon us his tender love and mercy. He longs for us to be at peace, to be happy in the light of his love. He has given us every good thing, so that we may seek him out and find him, and so that we might surrender our lives into his care. The Lord tells us through the prophet Isaiah that it is his will for all people to live in happiness and peace. He explains to us the true extent of his merciful love. He tells us that his love and mercy can overcome every evil, every sin. He tells us that not only will his merciful love overcome our sins, but that the forgiveness and grace that he offers us will be far above what we could ever expect. Let us turn to the Lord. Let us trust in his merciful love. Let our souls be filled to overflowing with the mercy and love of our God, who always offers us more than we could ever expect.

In His Image

(John 15:9-17)

"I have called you friends, because I have told you everything I have heard from my Father."

Through the life, death, and resurrection of Jesus, we have become his brothers and sisters. We have become the sons and daughters of the Father. We have become co-heirs with Jesus of the promises of God. Jesus reminds us that we have become reconciled to the Father through him. We have become friends of God through the salvation we have received through Jesus. Jesus tells us that we see the Father through him. We see the goodness and love of God through him. Our gift of faith grows as we follow the teaching and example of Jesus. We have received a special dignity of personhood through Jesus' love for us. Jesus tells us that we remain in him, remain reconciled to God, and live up to the dignity we enjoy by following his teachings and commandments. Jesus had made known the will of God for our lives, and he challenges us to understand and follow the path that has been laid out for us. Jesus is always there to give us help, first through the example of his own life, then through the example of the apostles, as well as the many men and women who have courageously followed the way of the Lord. Finally, Jesus gives us our pastors and leaders who continue to help us follow Jesus. Let us always strive to remain friends of Jesus, by loving one another, and by following the path that the Lord has set out for us.

Were Not Our Hearts Burning!

(Acts 15:7-21)

"He made no distinction between us and them, for by faith he
purified their hearts."

We are all one in the faith and the love that we share in Jesus' name. Our Lord came to earth to redeem each one of his beloved children, and every one of us is loved completely and unconditionally by our God. Every person has dignity in God. The Lord calls us to praise his name and be welcoming to all people as we walk this path of faith, and share with others the life we enjoy in Christ. In this passage the apostles came to grips with this truth of our faith. They came to understand that the salvation that came from Jesus was for all, and that it was following the teachings of Jesus, and the path on which he leads us that was important, and not where people came from or their former way of life. They were led by the Holy Spirit to be open to all of the ways, both old and new, that the Lord was working in the world. We are called to accept the way that the Holy Spirit continues to work in our lives and in our world. We are called to be welcoming to all of God's people and to understand that we are all equally loved by our God. Our God is good. His ways are wondrous and awesome. Let us strive to be open to all of his ways, and open to all of his people, as we seek to find our way to our everlasting reward in heaven.

In His Image

(John 1:29-34)

"Now I have seen and testified that he is the Son of God."

Our God loves us more than we can even imagine. He is Love itself. Yet, too many times we think of God more in terms of a judge rather than a loving Father. We think of God sitting up in heaven just waiting to trip us up, or keeping track of everything that we do wrong in our lives. The devil is hard at work trying to trick us into living in fear and dread of God's punishment. He does not want us to think of God in terms of love, but in terms of fear. St. John reminds us of the great love that God has for us. He has made us his children through his Son, Jesus. He has made us heirs with Jesus of his kingdom. He has freely given us the gift of his Son, though it is so much more than we deserve. All of this he has given out of love for us. He calls us to live in his love. He calls us to let him heal us of our fear and guilt. He calls on us to rely on his forgiveness and mercy. He calls us to freely choose him, to freely choose life over death, to freely choose light over darkness, to freely choose love over fear. He has given of himself totally to us, even in our sinfulness. Let us accept his love. Let us freely choose to love him.

Were Not Our Hearts Burning!

(1 John 3:1-2)

"See what love the Father has bestowed on us that we may be called the children of God."

Through Jesus we are reconciled to God, our Father. Through Jesus we are truly sons and daughters of God. We are truly the family of God. St. John tells us that because we are one family, we are called to love one another as family. Each person that we meet is a child of God, just as each of us is a child of God. Each person that we meet is loved by God with the same love that he has for each of us. We are all equally loved and cared for by our most gracious God. And so we must treat each other as family. We must care for each other with the same love that God shows us. We are called to use the holy family as an example. They lived in the love of God, always caring for each other, always teaching each other, always keeping each other in the light and love of God. We see in the holy family an example of humility. All three of them lived humbly, putting each other before themselves, and God before everything. We are called to that same humility, putting others before ourselves, and always walking humbly with our God. St. John reminds us that God is Love, and we who abide in love, abide in God, and he in us. Let us strive to live in, and share the love that God continually showers upon each of us.

In His Image

(Jeremiah 1:4-19)

The Word of the Lord came to me thus: before I formed you in the
womb I knew you."

Through the prophet Jeremiah our God acknowledges again his love
for every person, his love for the life that he creates. God tells Jeremiah
that he had a plan for him even before he was born, even before he was
formed in his mother's womb. God reminds us that he also had plans
for us before we were born. He tells us that he has known each one of us
even before he formed us in our mother's womb. Every single person is
known in that same way by God, even before that baby is formed. Every
life is known by God and is sacred to him. He tells us that it is his plan
for our lives that must be of paramount importance. He tells us that it
is his will, and not our will or convenience, that must be our priority as
Christian people. He asks us to have faith in him and his plan for our
lives, as well as his plan for all of life. He asks us to surrender our will
to him. It is in that surrender that our world will begin to heal from the
wounds that we have inflicted through our sinfulness. Let us praise God
in faith. Let us praise God in our obedience to his will.

Were Not Our Hearts Burning!

(John 21:1-19)

"He said to him, 'Feed my lambs.'"

We belong to the Lord. We are the sheep that he shepherds. In this passage Jesus questions Peter three times concerning his love for him, to remind Peter of the three times that he had denied him. In this questioning of Peter our Lord makes him whole, forgiving his sin of denial. Jesus also restates to Peter that he is to be the leader. He is the rock on which the church is to be built. We also notice that Jesus does not turn over the sheep to Peter. Jesus makes clear that all people are his own. He is our one true Shepherd. He is our King. In talking with Peter, Jesus claims each one of us as his own for all eternity. He commands Peter to feed "my" lambs, to feed "my" sheep. It is important for us to realize and remember that we have our dignity in our God. Our worth comes from being created in God's own image. No matter where we are in this journey of life, we still belong to the Lord. He loves us. We are a part of the body of his Son. Let us always remember that each of us is a special child of God. Let us thank the Lord for his goodness and grace in our lives. Let us treat each other with the dignity and worth that we all have in God.

In His Image

(Acts 13:16-42)

"After the congregation had dispersed, many Jews and worshipers
who were converts to Judaism followed Paul and Barnabas,
who spoke to them and urged them to remain faithful
to the grace of God."

God, our Father loves us with a deep and abiding love. He cares and provides for us. He pours out his grace upon us, and longs for us to receive it to good effect. He desires that we make use of his grace, and all that he provides for our welfare. Paul reminds his listeners, and us, to be faithful to the grace of God. The grace of God blesses and helps us. It brings us peace and joy. The grace of God will lead us to everlasting life. If, however, we are not open and faithful to the grace of God, we become lost. If we are not open and faithful to the grace of God, it is as if we are cut off from our lifeline. God calls us to work with his grace. He calls us to use all that he provides for our benefit. Let us make every effort to be always aware of the grace of God in our lives. Let us begin right now to use more effectively the many graces our God pours down upon us. Our God is all good and deserving of all of our faithfulness and praise.

2

A Lamp Unto My Feet

God's Word is power for our lives. It is enduring. By the Word of God we are guided in our lives. By the Word of God our souls are nourished. We gain the peace and security only our Lord can provide as we immerse ourselves in his Word and begin to live out in our lives the words he speaks.

Prayer

Almighty God, your Word gives us life. Your Word brings peace to our souls. We are secure in the power of your Word. Enlighten our minds as you speak your Word to us, so that we may experience you more fully. Root your Word in our hearts, so that we remain firm in you. Help us to be not only hearers of your Word, but doers of your Word, as we live out your plan for us.

Were Not Our Hearts Burning!

(Isaiah 55:10-11)

"For just as from the heavens the rain and snow come down and do
not return there till they have watered the earth, making it fertile
and fruitful, giving seed to him who sows and bread to him who
eats, so shall my word be that goes forth from my mouth; it shall not
return to me void, but shall do my will, achieving the end for which
I sent it."

The Word of God is food for our souls. Isaiah equates the importance
of the Word of God to our lives with the importance of the rain that
sustains the earth. The Word of the Lord sustains our lives. It sustains
us in times of trial and temptation. It fills us with hope and builds our
faith. The Word of God makes known to us the love of the Father for
each of us. It makes known the plan of God for our lives. The Word of
the Lord comes to us in many ways. It comes to us in Scripture, in prayer,
and through each other. The Lord calls us to be open to his Word in our
lives, so that our lives may be full. Let us open our hearts and minds to
the Word of God. Let us begin to hear him as he speaks to our souls. Let
us pray that we come to fully realize the power of God's Word in our
lives. Let us be fed and nourished by the Word of our Creator God.

A Lamp Unto My Feet

(Mark 1:21-28)

"The people were astonished at his teaching, for he taught them as one having authority and not as the scribes."

Jesus is the Word. He is the Way. He is the Truth. He is the Light. Jesus is all in all. In this passage from St. Mark's Gospel, Jesus proclaims the kingdom of God to the people. The people were convicted by the truth that he spoke, and were astonished that he spoke to them as no one else ever had. They realized that Jesus was anointed in the words he spoke. Jesus proclaims that same truth to us. He proclaims it in a way that will convict our hearts and change our lives. He asks only that we be open to receive his teaching, so that we may receive the blessing of his words, which are life to our souls. Jesus longs to speak to our hearts. He longs to change our lives and bring us closer to him. He longs to proclaim the kingdom of God to us in a most powerful way. We have heard and been touched by the words of charismatic and powerful speakers before. We know how those words can change us. Imagine how much more powerful the words of our God can be as he speaks them to us. The Lord asks that we pray for open hearts. He asks that we be properly disposed to hear his Word. He asks us to be ready as we read Scripture, pray, listen to our pastors, and as we share the Christ whom we know with each other. He promises that we, too, will be astonished by the power of his Word, the power of his spoken life.

Were Not Our Hearts Burning!

(Luke 24:13-35)

"Then they said to each other, 'Were not our hearts burning [within us] while he spoke to us on the way and opened the Scriptures to us?'"

The Lord makes himself known to us in many ways as we travel on this journey of faith. Mary Magdalene recognized Jesus, when in love he called her name. The two disciples on the road to Emmaus recognized Jesus in the breaking of the bread. Another way that God reveals himself to us is through his Word in Scripture. As Jesus broke open the Word for the two disciples, their hearts burned with the revelation of God and the understanding of Jesus as their Lord and Savior. The Lord wants us to know that burning in our hearts as we break open his Word in Scripture. He wants to teach and guide us by his Word. He wants to build our faith, and give us hope. He wants to comfort and console us. He wants to set our hearts and lives on fire for him. His Word can bring all of these gifts to us, and more, if we but open our minds and hearts to the power of his Word. As our God calls us to know him in his Word, let us take the opportunity, right now, to accept his invitation. Let us open our hearts to the guidance of the Holy Spirit, who will help us to understand. Let us strive to break open the Word of God more often, both in our individual prayer time and with our communities. Ours is a powerful and mighty God. He has so much for us, and many of the graces and gifts that he has for us begin in the power of his Word.

A Lamp Unto My Feet

(Matthew 13:10-17)

"The disciples approached him and said, 'Why do you speak to them in parables?'"

Jesus communicates to us in very different ways. Because we are all unique individuals, our Lord speaks to us in unique and varied ways. The disciples ask Jesus why he teaches them in one way and the people in another way. Jesus responds that he teaches everyone in the way that they will most easily understand, a way that will more readily enable them to believe. Jesus will continue to talk to each one of us in ways that will help us more easily understand. He will talk to each of us in ways that will help us more easily believe. Jesus is truly all things to all people. We are called to open our minds and prepare our hearts to hear the word of the Lord in our lives. Jesus tells us that when we are open to him he will speak to our hearts. He will lead us in the way of truth. He reminds us not to get discouraged if we do not understand everything, if we are confused by the complexity of theology, or if we do not seem to know as much as others. Jesus says that he will make clear all that we need to know. He will set our hearts and our lives on fire in a way that is unique to each of us. Jesus knows us better than we know ourselves. He knows how we learn. He knows what will stimulate our faith. He only asks that we be open so that he can speak to our hearts in the way that will be best for us.

Were Not Our Hearts Burning!

(Colossians 1:1-8)

"Just as in the whole world it is bearing fruit and growing, so also among you, from the day you heard it and came to know the grace of God in truth, as you learned it from Epaphras our beloved fellow slave, who is a trustworthy minister of Christ on your behalf and who also told us of your love in the Spirit."

The light of God will never grow dim. His Word and his truth will be spoken and shared throughout the world. St. Paul tells the people of Colossae that the Word of God cannot help but grow fruit. He tells them that the Word of God is being proclaimed every day and in every corner of the earth. It is also good for us to remember that the truth of God is resounding throughout the world. The message of the gospel is being preached and is bearing much fruit every day, everywhere in the world. Sometimes it can seem as if the Word of God is losing its foothold, especially in the secular societies in which we live. Religion is being pushed out of every area of our society. It can become discouraging. It is good to know that God's Word will never fail. The Good News will always be preached, and always bear fruit, because it is truth and light for all people. Let us strive to rejoice always in the power of God's Word. Let us strive to do all that we can to make sure that the Word of God can reach all people so that all can experience the love and light of Christ in their lives.

A Lamp Unto My Feet

(Luke 8:19-21)

"He said to them in reply, 'My mother and my brothers are those
who hear the Word of God and act on it.'"

In this passage the Lord tells us how important we are as members of
his mystical body. He tells us that as members of his body, we are his
brothers and sisters. We are one family in him. He also tells us what
we must do to remain alive in his body. He reminds us that as baptized
persons, we become members of his body, but we must continue to
hear God's Word in our lives. He then tells us that there is more than
just hearing his Word. He tells us that we must act on that Word. We
must live that Word in our lives. We must share that Word with others.
We must act and model every word that we hear from the Lord. The
act of living the Word can be difficult for us. It can be very hard to live
the Word of God in the world in which we live. We can readily see that
our world is becoming more secular. Separation of church and state is a
hot-button issue. And yet, the Lord tells us that we cannot separate our lives like that. He tells us that we must always live and
act on his Word in our lives. Let us pray for the grace to hear
well his Word, and to act boldly on the Word that we hear. Let us
pray for the courage to live fully the Word of the Lord, thereby
strengthening the body of Christ and bringing to fulfillment the
kingdom of God on earth.

Were Not Our Hearts Burning!

(Nehemiah 8:2-10, Luke 1:1-4)

"Since many have undertaken to compile a narrative of the events that have been fulfilled among us, just as those who were eyewitnesses from the beginning and ministers of the word have handed them down to us, I too have decided, after investigating everything accurately anew, to write it down in an orderly sequence for you, most excellent Theophilus, so that you may realize the certainty of the teachings you have received."

Our God has given us his inspired Word in Scripture to teach and guide us as we live our lives, as we strive to come closer to him and live in the light of his love. In the passage from the Old Testament book of Nehemiah, we read that the people wept as the law of the Lord was read to them. In Luke's Gospel we read how important he thought his own writing might be in helping others realize the certainty of Jesus' teachings. Our Lord continues to teach and guide us by his living Word in Scripture. He continues to build our faith, and bring us hope by the power of his Word. He constantly invites us to know him more intimately through his life and his Word to us in Scripture. He calls us to find strength and courage for our lives in the power of his Word. Let us pray for a new outpouring of the Holy Spirit in our lives, that we may hunger more and more for the Word of God in Scripture, and that we may be satisfied in our longing by coming closer to the Lord through his most powerful word.

A Lamp Unto My Feet

(James 1:19-27)

"Be doers of the word and not hearers only, deluding yourselves."

It is easy to say that we are Christian people. It is quite another to live that which we proclaim. That is what St. James is trying to explain to us. He reminds us that there is more to being a follower of Christ than just hearing his Word. He tells us that if we only hear the Word of God, and fail to live that Word in our lives, we will be easily led astray, for we will not know or fully understand the Word that we have received. But when we live that which we have received, it will become a part of us. We will understand more fully the life to which we are called in Christ. God's Word calls us to action. His Word calls us to live and share the gift of faith we have been given. God's Word calls us to be open to the prompting of the Holy Spirit, who will guide us and spur us to action. God's Word calls us to be always open so that he can touch our hearts and our lives, and then touch others through the example of our lives. Let us pray that we are always more than just hearers of God's Word. Let us pray for the grace to be doers of God's Word, a Word that will change our lives, as well as the lives of those to whom we reach out. God's Word is light and salvation, joy and peace, and it is only when we act upon it that we can begin to truly experience the fullness of his Word.

Were Not Our Hearts Burning!

(Luke 4:14-22)

"And all spoke highly of him and were amazed at the gracious words
that came from his mouth."

In this passage St. Luke tells us about the beginning of Jesus' ministry. He recounts for us the visit of Jesus to the synagogue in the town where he grew up. The people listened and were amazed at what he said. They felt that he had spoken with the authority of God. Yet they had a difficult time believing in what he said and following him because he was someone they knew. He was only the son of a carpenter. How could one of their own have the authority to teach and lead the people? They would wait and listen to someone who was of a better class. Of course we know that they missed out on a wonderful opportunity to share in the love and peace of God. Sometimes, in our own lives, we dismiss a chance to share in the love and peace of God, because we, too, are quick to discount the messenger. We, too, often dismiss the Word of God that we hear or the example of God's love that we encounter from the people that are closest to us, our families, our own pastors, people in our own communities. We are more open to people we don't know, or people who have a reputation for preaching and teaching. We are called to be open to Jesus in everyone we know and meet. Jesus can work through all of us. It is when we are totally open to the Lord in all people, and in all things, that we benefit most from the love and peace of God.

A Lamp Unto My Feet

(John 8:31-42)

"Jesus then said to those Jews who believed in him, 'If you remain in my word, you will truly be my disciples, and you will know the truth, and the truth will set you free.'"

In this passage Jesus gives us a teaching about what we need to do to be true followers. He tells us that as long as we remain in his Word, we can do nothing less than continue to follow him more closely, and thereby be his disciples. We are called to make God's Word the foundation of our lives. We are called to read and study his Word in Scripture, and then, as we are enlightened by the Holy Spirit, live out the Word in our lives. Jesus promises that as we remain in his Word, we will know the truth through the power of the Holy Spirit. He then promises that as we come to understand the truth, the truth will set us free. True freedom can only come in the truth of the Lord as revealed in his Word to us. Let us pray that we have a hunger for the truth of God's Word. Let us pray that as we read and study God's Word in Scripture, we receive new gifts of understanding and wisdom through the power of the Holy Spirit. Let us live in the truth of God's Word, and in that truth find the freedom the Lord promises.

Were Not Our Hearts Burning!

(Acts 13:44-52)

"On the following sabbath almost the whole city gathered to hear
the word of the Lord. When the Jews saw the crowds, they were
filled with jealousy and with violent abuse contradicted
what Paul said."

When the Word of God is preached in the power and anointing of the
Holy Spirit, hearts and minds are changed. People are brought to the
Lord. We read how powerful the Word of the Lord can be as almost the
whole city was drawn to hear Paul preach the Word of God. The disciples
were often successful in getting people to listen, and as they listened
God was able to change their hearts. We are called to make ready the
hearts of others by the goodness of our lives and the testimony of God's
power in our lives, so that as they hear the Word of God he can change
hearts and minds. So often this is not as easy as it might seem. As hearts
and minds are changed, the threat to others' beliefs becomes stronger,
and they react with force, and even at times with "violent abuse." Our
Lord calls us to persevere in his call to us to share our lives with others,
so that he can touch hearts and change minds. Nothing will stop the
Word of the Lord. Our God tells us that his Word will not return to him
until it has accomplished all that it was sent to do. We, as Christians,
are called to be facilitators of that most holy Word of God.

A Lamp Unto My Feet

(Luke 24:13-35)

"With that their eyes were opened and they recognized him, but he
vanished from their sight."

Through the Word of the Lord, with the Holy Spirit as our guide,
our hearts burn as we read and study sacred Scripture. We are fed by
that Word. We are nourished by that Word. We grow in our faith and
our relationship with the Lord in that Word. The Word of God is our
lifeblood. In the breaking of the bread in Holy Communion, we are
equally fed, equally nourished, equally helped in our faith and our relationship with the Lord. The body and blood of Jesus is also our life
blood. It is interesting that the two disciples first recognized Jesus in the
breaking of the bread, and then realized that they had also recognized him
in the word of Scripture. This passage is certainly a lesson for us. We are
called to come and find the Lord in the sacrament of his body and blood,
as well as in his Word in Scripture. Our Lord tells us that we will always
find him, we will always recognize him, and we will always be blessed in
sacrament and Scripture. Let us thank the Lord for being always present
to us, as we continually search for him. Let us thank him for his gifts of
sacrament and Scripture.

Were Not Our Hearts Burning!

(1 John 1:1-4)

"What was from the beginning, what we have heard, what we have
seen with our eyes, what we looked upon and touched with our
hands concerns the word of life–for the life was made visible; we
have seen it and testify to it and proclaim to you the eternal life that
was with the Father and was made visible to us–what we have seen
and heard we proclaim now to you, so that you too may have fellowship with us; for our fellowship is with the Father and with his Son,
Jesus Christ."

St. John's letter fills us with hope. The strength of St. John, through the
power of the Holy Spirit, strengthens us. The awesome power and love
of God jump off the page and into our hearts. We are truly exhorted
and empowered by St. John to embrace the power of God, in Jesus, and
strive to make Jesus visible in our own lives as we continue our spiritual
journey on this earth. These verses from the first letter of St. John are
a testament to the power that Scripture can have in our lives. They are
a testament to the power of the Holy Spirit, with which the evangelists
were blessed. Indeed, the power of Scripture can and will change our
lives if we are open to it. Let us pray that the Holy Spirit bless us with
new insight as we read God's Word in Scripture. Let us pray that as we
are open to the power of God in Scripture, our lives are changed and
we are empowered to live holy lives as God becomes more visible to us
and we come closer to the Lord in our lives.

3

Awesome In His Power

Our Lord continues to act in our lives and in our world. As we are able to open our hearts to him, he is able to change our circumstances, heal us, and work wonders and miracles in our lives.

Prayer

Mighty God, open our hearts to the wonder of your power in our lives. Strengthen our belief in your healing power as you act to bring us closer to you. Open our eyes to the wonders and miracles that you continue to work in our lives and in our world.

Were Not Our Hearts Burning!

(Isaiah 35:4-7)

"Streams will burst forth in the desert, and rivers in the steppe."

The power of God to change our hearts and our lives is awesome. He is able to change our circumstances no matter what they are. He is a God of miracles. The prophet Isaiah paints a beautiful picture of the power of our God to effect changes in his creation. He tells us that those things which we cannot even imagine changing can be changed by the power of God. The most desolate barren place can be changed into a place of beauty. The most desolate lonely heart can be changed into a beautiful happy heart. Just so, our souls can be changed by the power of God. No matter where we are in our lives, no matter what we have done, our God can make us into a beautiful new creation. He can and will forgive our sins and shower his mercy upon us. He can and will change our fear, loneliness, and desolation into peace and joy. In his love for us he can bring a happiness that we cannot, at this time, imagine. Let us surrender our lives to the power of the Lord. Let us open our hearts to his love and power, that as the streams will burst forth in the desert, his grace will burst forth in us, and our lives will be changed forever into the beautiful creation our God has intended that we be.

Awesome In His Power

(Daniel 1:1-21)

"He acceded to this request, and tested them for ten days; after ten
days they looked healthier and better fed than any of the young men
who ate at the royal table."

In this passage Daniel places his full trust in the Lord, even in the midst
of what everyone else thought to be impossible. Daniel trusted that the
Lord would find a way to bring about the desired result if he followed
God's plan for his life. Indeed, we read that the result was even better
than even Daniel could have hoped for. Our Lord calls us to trust in his
will for our lives. He calls us to trust in him, even when we think things
are impossible. Daniel knew and teaches us that nothing is impossible
for God. Even though we say that we understand God can do anything,
we are still hesitant to place our lives in his hands. We still want control
for ourselves. We still do not trust in the power of God enough to take
the step of submitting our whole life to him. Let us pray that we are
strengthened in our resolve to trust the Lord. Let us pray that we grow
each day in the confidence of God's power in our lives. Let us begin
today to be more aware of the times we fail to submit our lives to God's
power and strive to trust him more to know what is best for us.

Were Not Our Hearts Burning!

(Mark 5:21-43)

"She said, 'If I but touch his clothes, I shall be cured.'"

The woman in this passage provides an example of great faith in the power of Jesus. We also read how Jesus rewarded the woman's faith by curing her as she touched his clothes. We are called to that same vision of Jesus' power in our lives. We are called to realize that we are empowered in Jesus. We have everything we need in Jesus. He is our peace and joy. He is our healer. It is in Jesus that we find the answer to every problem and concern. It is in Jesus that we have our very lives. Jesus is keenly interested in every aspect of our lives. He is interested in everything in which we are interested. Jesus invites us to come to him for his healing power, as did the woman in the Gospel. He invites us to come to him for help in those areas of our lives that are so difficult for us, those areas in which we are in such need of his intercession. He wants us to know that when we do come to him, he will change our circumstances. With one touch of his healing hands we are healed. Too often we believe that Jesus can heal, but we don't believe that he will heal us. In our weakness of faith, we believe that the healing power of Jesus is for someone else. We feel that we are unworthy. We have faith for others, but not for ourselves. Jesus calls us to a new level of faith in his power. He calls us to believe in his love and care for us. He calls us to trust that in his great love for us he wants only what is best for us, and that when we come to him he can and will heal our lives and bring us into the depth of his love. In his love, and by his touch, we are healed and renewed.

Awesome In His Power

(Matthew 1:1-17)

"The book of the genealogy of Jesus Christ, the son of David, the son of Abraham."

This passage is a recitation of the genealogy of Jesus. St. Matthew traces the lineage of Jesus' human family back through the ages to King David, and finally to Abraham. In this genealogy, St. Matthew shows us that Jesus is truly a man. He shows with his detailing of the lineage of Jesus, that Jesus truly is the culmination of God's promise to send a Savior born in the line of King David. The tracing of Jesus' family tree shows us even more about the power and majesty of our God. As we read the names of those in Jesus' line, we notice that Jesus had many different types of relatives. Some were very good and some were very bad, and yet the plan of God was never thwarted. He was able to produce a good end out of both the good and the bad. God calls us to understand that he can and will bring about good in any situation. He tells us that we must never despair, that we must always strive to do his will. He calls us to accept his will for our lives, and to rejoice in any trials that we must endure, to rejoice wherever we are on our walk with him, because he will bring good from all of our trials. He will bring good from all of our suffering and hardship. In the genealogy of Jesus, we learn the lesson that God's will must always prevail. Let us pray to be always open to the plan of God, and that we always have the strength to persevere in that plan, relying always on the power and majesty of God.

Were Not Our Hearts Burning!

(Mark 8:22-26)

"Then he laid hands on his eyes a second time and he saw clearly;
his sight was restored and he could see everything distinctly."

We know that the Lord heals us in many ways. As we examine our lives, we come to realize the numerous ways that we have been healed by the Lord. We have known the touch of the Lord in every area of our lives—physical, emotional, and spiritual. Mark recounts the story of the healing of a blind man. The Lord continued to be present to him, to touch him, and to work with him until he was completely healed. The Lord works the same way in our lives. Many times the healing of the Lord in our lives is gradual. The Lord heals us in the way that he knows is best for us. He continually works with us until we are completely healed. The Lord touches our lives and heals us as we can accept it. We are called to be open to the presence and the action of the Lord in our lives. He asks us to be responsive to the way in which he touches and heals us. We are also called to examine our lives so as to be always aware of the many ways that the Lord is touching and healing us. We are asked to trust the Lord, who in his goodness and love continues to provide for us and heal us in all of the ways we need to be healed so that we are able to come closer to him every day of our lives.

Awesome In His Power

(1 Samuel 2:1-10, Luke 1:46-56)

"My heart exults in the Lord, my horn is exalted in my God."

These passages, one from the Old Testament, and one from the New Testament, reflect the majesty and power of our God. We read of God's majesty as he raises up two women and blesses them with the announcement of children. Both women heard the Word of God and opened their lives to his plan for them. Each woman comes to understand the greatness of the Lord in the announcements that are brought to them. Each accepts the Word of God humbly, and each is blessed in her humility. Each of them exults in the Lord and speaks of God's omnipotent power and never-ending love. We must also come to know and to understand the power of God in our lives. It is good for us to reflect on the prayers uttered by both of these women as they were blessed by the Lord. They knew that they were helpless on their own, but also knew that through the power and might of our God, nothing is impossible. Let us pray that we, too, live humbly in our lives, relying on the grace and love of God for all of our needs. Let us put far from us the pride that so often keeps us from all the Lord wants for us. Let us rejoice always in the Lord, living in his plan for us, and returning, by the example of our lives, the love he so bountifully showers upon us.

Were Not Our Hearts Burning!

(John 20:19-31)

"Now Jesus did many other signs in the presence of [his] disciples
that are not written in this book. But these are written that you may
[come to] believe that Jesus is the Messiah, the Son of God, and that
through this belief you may have life in his name."

St. John reminds us that the Lord is a living God, a God who continues
to act powerfully in our lives and in our world. He reminds us that the
Gospels are not the end, but the beginning in the constant action of
our God among his people. Our Lord worked many signs and wonders
in the presence of his disciples, in order that we who have come after
them might know the power and majesty of the Lord. But as we come
to believe in him, we will see much more. We will experience our Lord
in new and unique ways. We will come to know him as a living and
eternal God, not as just a figure in history. The miracles of the Gospels
are the same miracles that Jesus continues to perform among his people
today, and will continue to perform among his people tomorrow. He is
always powerfully active and present to those who believe. He is truly
a living God. He is a God who continues to love us, to protect us, and
to guide us on this journey of life on earth, which leads to eternal life
with him in heaven.

Awesome In His Power

(Isaiah 41:13-20, Matthew 11:15)

"Whoever has ears ought to hear."

The Old Testament Book of Isaiah is filled with prophecies of God's love, mercy, power, and majesty. The vision of the world, through the eyes of the prophet Isaiah, shows the desire of our God to redeem his people, to change their lot, and to rescue them from the power of evil. Isaiah sees the deserts being changed into marshlands. He sees all of those places we consider barren and wasted changed into life-sustaining, life-nurturing, beautiful places. Through the power of the gift of his Son, our world is changed. Our lives have been saved. Beauty has replaced the desolate and barren wastelands of our lives. Strength has replaced weakness. Our lives have become like the trees that Isaiah mentions, growing strong and tall, nourished by the life-giving water of God's grace. We may still see ugliness in our world, but we are called to rise above that, because we live in the power of Jesus. St. Matthew tells us that if we have ears we ought to hear. Indeed, we must open our eyes and ears more fully to the life-giving gift that we have in Jesus. We have been redeemed. The victory has been won. Let us truly hear, truly see that we are changed by the power of God.

Were Not Our Hearts Burning!

(Acts 3:11-26)

"And by faith in his name, this man, whom you see and know, his name has made strong, and the faith that comes through it has given him this perfect health, in the presence of all of you."

The name of Jesus is so powerful. In his name people are changed. In his name people are healed. In his name wonders and miracles abound. In his name people of faith continue to bring healing and consolation to his people. Peter recounts to his listeners the facts of the healing that they had just witnessed. A man who was crippled was healed by the power of Jesus' name. Jesus had used Peter and John to cure the man, and through the wonder of that healing many were added to the church. The Lord calls each of us to be aware of the wonders and miracles worked in our midst. He continues to strengthen our faith through his power and majesty. He then calls us to share that faith, to share that power, by being open to his call to service. As we serve each other, as we pray for each other, as we are used by the Lord to bring his healing and consolation to each other, the majesty of the Lord is made manifest. The name of the Lord is glorified, and many more will come to believe.

Awesome In His Power

(John 5:1-16)

"When Jesus saw him lying there and knew that he had been ill for a long time, he said to him, 'Do you want to be well?'"

In this passage we read of a man who had been ill for thirty-eight years. It seems curious that Jesus would ask him if he wanted to be healed. After all, he was sitting at the pool and had been coming there for a long time. Yet, Jesus still asked him if he wanted to be well. We know that Jesus is always close to us. He is always there with his healing touch for our lives. He is always there to heal us in the many ways he knows that we need to be healed. However, many times Jesus asks us the same question he asked the sick man, and asks that we really think about it. Do we really want to be healed, or do we put up barriers to the healing power of Jesus in our lives? Would we rather be in a situation with which we are familiar rather than be healed and possibly begin a new way of life? Would we rather complain about our weaknesses than be healed and be strong in the Lord, where there may be more demands on us to live more bold Christian lives? These are some of the questions our Lord calls us to reflect on as we come to him for healing. The Lord longs to heal us and to bring us into communion with himself, and so he asks us, "Do you want to be well?"

Were Not Our Hearts Burning!

(2 Kings 5:1-15)

"But his servants came up and reasoned with him. 'My Father,' they
said, 'if the prophet had told you to do something extraordinary,
would you not have done it?'"

This is the story of the cure of the army commander, Naaman, from the
disease of leprosy. Naaman had heard of a powerful prophet in Israel,
and so went to him when all else had failed so that he might be cured.
Elisha, the prophet, told him to go wash in the Jordan River and he
would be cured. Naaman could not believe that something so simple
could possibly cure him, especially after all he had tried in his homeland.
He was about to go home, when his servants persuaded him to comply
with Elisha's command. Naaman did comply and he was healed. Many
times in our own lives we fail to be open to the many and varied ways
in which the Lord acts in our lives. Sometimes, while we are waiting
for a big miracle, we fail to be open to the many ordinary ways the Lord
works in our lives. He works through our families, through our doctors,
and others with whom we interact every day. He works in the ordinary
events of our lives. He heals us through his Word, his sacraments, and
through the prayers that we say, and those that are said for us every day
and may be taken for granted. We are called to be always open to the
ordinary action of the Lord in our lives, as well as the extraordinary. Let
us come to know that the Lord is with us every day and in every way.

Awesome In His Power

(Isaiah 40:1-11)

"Comfort, give comfort to my people, says your God."

Surely through the birth of Jesus, our Savior, God has given all human-ity comfort. As Christian people we are experiencing this comfort every day in our lives. The birth of Jesus has changed the plight of humanity forever. We are now members of one body, members of the mystical body of Christ. We are truly sons and daughters of our most gracious God, through Jesus. The darkness and the wasteland of which Isaiah speaks, are banished in the life and power of Jesus. We are made whole in his birth, life, death, resurrection, and ascension into heaven. Through our baptism into his life, we receive his strength and power. In baptism we are buried with Christ, and die to ourselves, and are reborn in him to live our lives as a sacrifice to God. The sacrament of baptism gives us comfort and a certain hope that we will one day live with Jesus for all eternity in the presence of Almighty God. Let us rejoice in our mighty and merciful God. Let us rejoice in his great love for us. Let us rejoice in the life of our Savior, Jesus, who brings comfort to our lives, as well as the promise of eternal life. Let us pray for the grace to understand and experience every day the comfort and the power we have in the Lord.

4

BLESSED ARE YOU WHO BELIEVE

Our faith is the foundation of our Christian lives. It is by God's most precious gift of faith that we are saved. It is by faith that we come to know and experience our God. It is our faith that gives us strength and courage to live brave and holy lives in this imperfect world. It is our faith that allows us to open our hearts to receive the grace and gifts the Lord showers upon his people.

PRAYER

Most gracious Lord, thank you for the precious gift of faith that you have given us. Nourish the seed of faith that you have so lovingly planted within us. Strengthen our faith and trust in you. Help us to protect and care for this beautiful gift, and help us in our unbelief.

Were Not Our Hearts Burning!

(1 Thessalonians 1:1-10)

"For our gospel did not come to you in word alone, but also in
power and in the Holy Spirit and [with] much conviction."

It is God himself who gives us the wonderful gift of faith. He works
through his people to deliver the message, but it is he who gives the
gift. St. Paul reminds us of this truth. He reminds us that although we
hear and share the word with others, our faith is much more powerful,
because the Lord gives the gift. He has given this gift, and in this gift is
power because he is the giver. He has also given us the gift of the Holy
Spirit, who nourishes our faith as well as teaches and guides us. The
Holy Spirit confirms the gift we have been given. He strengthens our
faith. Coming to know and understand the power of the gift we have
received, we are called to open our hearts to the prompting of the Holy
Spirit. We are called to remain firm in our faith by relying on the Holy
Spirit to teach and guide us, by relying on the Holy Spirit to build us up
in the life and love of God. In the power of the Holy Spirit, we will come
to know the value of the gift of faith, which we have been given. We
will grow steadily stronger in our faith, so that we will be more able to
withstand trial and temptation in our lives, and one day join our Father
in heaven for all eternity.

Blessed Are You Who Believe

(Exodus 32:15-24, Matthew 13:31-35)

"It is the smallest of all seeds, yet when full-grown it is the largest of plants."

Our Lord teaches us that the seed of our faith can be very fragile. This is especially true when the seed is small, when our faith is struggling to grow. That tiny seed of faith must be protected. We must guard and nurture it so that it may grow, and in that growth be impervious to those things which would cause damage. The trials and temptations, which abound in our society, can have a devastating effect on our faith if we are not careful. We can easily find ourselves being led away from the Lord and the seed of our faith crushed. In the book of Exodus we read that the Israelites often succumbed to the trials they faced. Their faith was weakened. They forgot the works of the Lord, and in their weakness and lack of faith they turned from him. When Moses did not return from the mountain, the seed of their faith was not properly nurtured. They were ripe for the wiles of the devil and they sinned. We must always keep the light of our faith burning brightly through the continued practice of our faith. We must stay close to the Lord in his Word and in his sacraments so that we will remain strong against the devil and the seed of our faith has an opportunity to grow from the smallest of seeds into the largest of plants.

Were Not Our Hearts Burning!

(Matthew 13:44-46)

"When he finds a pearl of great price, he goes and sells all that he
has and buys it."

The Lord continually challenges us to value our faith above all else in
our lives. He continually reminds us that in our faith, we have one of the
greatest gifts from God that we will ever be given. It is through our faith
that we have come to know his Son, Jesus, and the salvation he has won
for us. It is through our faith that we have been able to open our hearts
to the power of the Holy Spirit. Everything of importance that we have
comes from the gift of faith, which we have received from our Father.
In faith, we are members of the kingdom of God. We are members of
the body of Christ. Jesus commands that we value above all else the gift
of faith, which we have been given. He tells us that when we put our
faith first, we will find happiness and contentment, even in the midst
of the stress we face every day. Let us pray that we always put our faith
and the kingdom of God first in our lives. Let us pray that through the
help of the Holy Spirit we are able to correctly prioritize all the aspects
of our hectic lives.

Blessed Are You Who Believe

(Mark 9:14-29)

"Then the boy's father cried out, 'I do believe, help my unbelief!'"

In this passage Jesus drives out a demon who had tenaciously possessed a young boy. The apostles were not able to effect the cure, but Jesus called on the boy's father to have faith. Many times in our lives we are called to have faith in the power and majesty of Jesus. We are called to have faith despite all of the evidence or the weight of public opinion to the contrary. Jesus continues to remind us that there are no impossibilities for those who have faith. And yet, we find that all too often our faith is weak. Let us pray, as did the father of the boy, for Jesus' help in our unbelief. Let us call on him for strength and a strong faith in those situations, which seem so hopeless to us. Let us call on him for the courage to persevere in our faith and hope in him. He is our God, and he will never abandon us. He will always be our help and protection. He is loving and caring, and most surely deserves all of our faith and trust.

Were Not Our Hearts Burning!

(John 16:29-33)

"Behold, the hour is coming and has arrived when each of you will
be scattered to his own home and you will leave me alone."

The apostles must have been surprised to hear Jesus tell them that they would not stand by him. They had pledged their faith and loyalty to Jesus and told him that they had come to believe that he was the Christ. Yet, here is Jesus telling them that their faith would be shaken and they would turn their backs on him. We know, of course, that it did happen just as Jesus had said it would. When Jesus was arrested, the apostles ran away. The apostles had seen all that Jesus had done. They had seen the majesty and the glory of God in Jesus, and yet their faith was still weak. They still turned away from the Lord. In this world of sin and temptation, our faith can be very delicate. We can easily find ourselves turning away from the Lord. The Lord reminds us that we must constantly seek to nurture and build our faith. He reminds us, too, that we must pray constantly that we might be strong in our hour of temptation. Finally, Jesus draws our attention to the fact that although the apostles did run away, they came back to him. They came back and received the forgiveness and mercy of God and continued the work of the Lord. The Lord calls us to receive his forgiveness and mercy in our times of weakness that we may be made whole in him.

Blessed Are You Who Believe

(2 Corinthians 11:1-11)

"For if someone comes and preaches another Jesus than the one we preached, or if you receive a different spirit from the one you received or a different gospel from the one you accepted, you put up with it well enough."

We have been blessed to receive the true word of God and in understanding through faith the way of the Lord. St. Paul reminds his hearers, and us, that we must zealously guard our faith. We must always be aware that there are many errant theologies, which continue to crop up in our society, theologies which may seem easier or novel in their approach. St. Paul admonishes us against falling for anything other than the true message that we have received, no matter what the temptation. He tells us that these errant theologies will always be with us, a constant temptation for us, but that we must stay strong in our faith by remembering always that our faith has come from Jesus himself. St. Paul tells us that to stay strong we must stay active in our faith. We must never become lax in practicing our faith, for it is in laxity that we can be swayed by false teachings. We must also continue to learn more about our faith, for it is in lack of knowledge that we may become tempted by false teachings. Our faith is a wonderful gift from God. His way is a blessing for our lives. Let us never lose our way. Let us always remain strong in Jesus.

Were Not Our Hearts Burning!

(Matthew 8:5-17)

"The centurion said in reply, 'Lord, I am not worthy to have you enter under my roof; only say the word and my servant will be healed.'"

The centurion provides us with an excellent example of faith from which we can learn. It is our nature as human beings to want to see before we believe. We are sometimes slow to believe things which we cannot fully verify. Yet, here we have an example of a person with total faith in the authority of the Lord. He acknowledges Jesus' authority over him and over the forces of sickness. He acknowledges Jesus as Lord by proclaiming that he is not worthy to have Jesus come into his home, but shows faith and courage by coming to the Lord even in his unworthiness. We know that we are also unworthy. We also acknowledge Jesus as Lord. We know that he is our healer. We know that he holds power over heaven and earth. Jesus calls us to have the faith of the centurion. He calls us to have faith in his power to heal and change our lives. He calls us to come to him with courage and in faith, even in our unworthiness, comfortable in the knowledge that he loves us and desires to help and heal us.

Blessed Are You Who Believe

(Matthew 12:38-42)

"Then some of the scribes and Pharisees said to him, 'Teacher, we
wish to see a sign from you.'"

How many times in our lives have we, like the scribes and Pharisees,
wished to see a sign from the Lord? How many times has doubt crept
into our minds and our faith become weak, and we thought, as Thomas
did, that we must touch the nail marks and put our fist into the hole in
Jesus' side? Jesus admonishes us it is truly in weakness that we ask for
these signs. He reminds us that we have already seen many signs and
wonders. He tells us that he continues to work signs and wonders, even
in our own age. Jesus encourages us to open the eyes of our faith. He
has given us this wonderful gift so that we might believe. He teaches
that we must exercise the gift of our faith as we come to know him in
his Word, and through each other. Our Lord continues to give us all we
need to believe in him, to know that his Word and his teachings are true.
Let us pray that our faith be strengthened in Jesus by the power of the
Holy Spirit. Let us pray that we will continue to build each other up in
faith through the example of our lives.

Were Not Our Hearts Burning!

(Luke 4:16-30)

"Again there were many lepers in Israel during the time of Elisha the
prophet; yet not one of them was cleansed, but only
Naaman the Syrian."

Many of us have been Christians all of our lives. We have known the
Lord for as long as we can remember. Jesus reminds us that we must
always be on guard so as to not take for granted the wonderful gift we
have in our faith. The examples Jesus gives us from this passage in St.
Luke's Gospel are especially pointed toward those who might forget the
power of faith. Jesus warns us that the more familiar our faith becomes,
the more we have to guard against complacency. We are given examples
of people who were the closest to God, missing out on his blessings,
while others who were less familiar with the power and majesty of God
were healed because they were open to his action in their lives. Many
times we experience the same things. We marvel at the energy and the
strong faith that are so apparent in those who are just new in the faith
and have newly accepted Jesus as their Lord and Savior. Jesus tells us
that we must always strive to retain that energy in our faith. We must
always keep our faith new. We must always keep our hearts open to the
action of God in our lives. We keep our faith alive by living it every day.
We keep it alive by constantly communicating with the Lord in prayer
and opening our hearts to his Word. Let us pray that our faith be always
vibrant and strong, that we may be always open to the majesty and power
of God in our lives.

Blessed Are You Who Believe

(Luke 10:17-24)

"At that very moment he rejoiced [in] the Holy Spirit and said, 'I give you praise, Father, Lord of heaven and earth, for although you have hidden these things from the wise and the learned you have revealed them to the childlike.'"

It is by faith that we journey with the Lord. It is in trusting him that we are strong. Jesus praises God for his plan. In his prayer, he reminds us that we must always praise the Lord and be thankful for the gift of faith he has given us. He reminds us that our faith will grow in proportion to our praise of God's wisdom. Jesus teaches us how much more important our faith is in knowing our Father, rather than trying to comprehend him through our human intelligence. It is God's plan that we live our life by faith. It is his plan that we trust him with all of our needs. That is why it is so important for us to continue to strive to build our faith and trust in the Lord, even as we tend toward independence in our lives. Let us pray to be always open to all of the gifts the Lord has for us through a strong faith and trust in him. Let us pray for the peace and joy of the Lord that comes from a true childlike faith in the majesty, power, and wisdom of our God.

Were Not Our Hearts Burning!

(Mark 4:26-34)

"He said, 'This is how it is with the kingdom of God; it is as if a man were to scatter seed on the land and would sleep and rise night and day and the seed would sprout and grow, he knows not how.'"

This passage from St. Mark's Gospel reflects the true mystery of our faith. Jesus compares our faith and its growth to seed which a farmer plants. If the farmer takes care of the seeds and plants, if he nurtures them, then he must have faith that they will grow into mature plants, which he can then harvest for his benefit. Jesus tells us that it is the same for our faith. If we provide good ground for the seed and nurture that seed by a good life, then we must have faith that God will make that seed grow and mature. We must come to realize that God will care for us and supply whatever we need to make our faith flourish. Jesus does admonish us, however, that if we fail to provide good ground, if we fail to nurture and care for the seed of faith given to us, the seed will not grow, but will be trampled or blown away. Let us pray for the grace we need to guard and nurture our seed of faith. Let us pray for the wisdom to trust God to provide all that we need, and that by his grace our faith will flourish as he continues to love and care for us.

Blessed Are You Who Believe

(James 1:1-11)

"But he should ask in faith, not doubting, for the one who doubts is
like a wave of the sea that is driven and tossed about by the wind."

St. James reminds us of how important it is that we never doubt the
goodness, love, and power of the Lord. He compares those who doubt
to waves that are tossed every which way and driven by the wind, with
no clear path. All of us have doubted at one time or another, and so we
know that the comparison St. James makes is a valid one. The times when
we have doubted are the times we feel that we have no control. We feel
lost and alone. St. James reminds us that it is in our times of doubt that
our faith must take over. It is our faith that will sustain us and keep us
strong. It is in our faith that we find the courage to ask our Lord for his
help and protection. When we allow our faith to grow and drive out the
little doubts that plague us, we will be living the confident life to which
we are called by our gracious God. Let us pray that the Lord bless us
with a growing faith. Let us respond to the faith that we have been given
so that when trials do appear, our faith will be strong enough to sustain
us. In faith, let us pray that we will always live confidently, knowing that
the Lord will always be with us.

Were Not Our Hearts Burning!

(James 2:14-26)

"What good is it, my brothers, if someone says he has faith but does not have works?"

St. Paul tells us that we are saved by faith. He tells us when we believe Jesus is Lord and that he died for our sins, that faith in him will be our salvation. St. James fleshes out for us what our faith must entail. He exhorts us to strengthen and boldly live our faith through good works. We who believe in the Lord can testify to the truth of St. James' question to us concerning faith and works. The two are inseparable. We know that in our belief in the lordship of Jesus, we can do nothing less than praise him in the works that we do. We can do nothing less than proclaim and share the loving salvation of Jesus with others. We can do nothing less than all that we can to provide for all of God's children who are suffering or in need. We must fully live out our faith by following the example of the object of that faith, Jesus himself. In his life on earth, Jesus showed his love for all people through his good works in the name of our heavenly Father. We certainly can do no less. So, when we say that we believe, when we say that we have faith, let us live out that faith in the praise of our God in heaven and in the example of Jesus, our Savior, by loving and working for all of our brothers and sisters in Christ.

Blessed Are You Who Believe

(Luke 16:19-31)

"Then Abraham said, 'If they will not listen to Moses and the prophets, neither will they be persuaded if someone should rise from the dead.'"

This passage from St. Luke's Gospel is a sobering story of a rich man who lived his life according to worldly ways, and then is condemned to the fire when he dies. He begs for a drop of water, but is denied because he failed to provide relief for those who begged from him during his life on earth. He asks father Abraham to send someone to warn his family of the error of their ways, but Abraham tells him that they certainly would not believe anyone else since they had not believed the people and the signs that God had provided. The Lord has given us ample signs and many guideposts to help us on our journey. He has given us the gift of his Son, the gift of the Holy Spirit, the gift of sacred Scripture, and continues to work signs and wonders in our world. Yet, sometimes our faith still flags. We want still more proof of the truths of our God. We want still more signs as we fail to stay aware of all that the Lord has already provided. God tells us that we have been given everything we require to remain strong in our faith. He tells us that if we do not believe with all that he has done and continues to do, nothing more could convince us. Let us ponder the truths of this passage from Scripture. Let us take comfort from our faith, which God continues to build in us by his most gracious love and mercy.

Were Not Our Hearts Burning!

(John 14:23-29)

"And now I have told you this before it happens, so that when it happens you may believe."

Jesus wanted to give the apostles every reason to believe in him. He wanted them to know and believe that he was their Lord and Savior. Many of the teachings and ways of Jesus were foreign to the way of life with which the apostles were familiar. His love, his peace, and his mercy available to everyone were very new and different. Jesus wanted to tell the apostles what was going to happen because it was so difficult to understand, and he wanted them to believe it. The peace of the Lord, the way he loves every person, even his enemies, and the tremendous mercy he shows us are all very different from our earthly expectations. It may be hard for us to believe that the promises of the Lord, and his desire that we live peaceful, joyful, and full lives in him, are possible, even as the world pulls us in different directions, except that he has told us all that will happen so that we, too, may believe. He has made himself known to us, even though we cannot see him, through his Word and the Holy Spirit, so that we may remain strong in our faith. Our Lord calls us to know and to study his Word and his promises, so that when temptations occur, as they always will, we will be able to persevere in faith, living peacefully and joyfully in his love.

Blessed Are You Who Believe

(John 20:19-31)

"Blessed are those who have not seen and have believed."

The story of "doubting" Thomas is a familiar one, which recounts Thomas' lack of faith in the resurrection of Jesus. Thomas was a person who experienced doubt like many of us. He wanted proof and was slow to believe until he had that proof. The other apostles, who had witnessed to him what they themselves had seen, did not sway Thomas. Many people witness to us, and yet there are many times when we still find it difficult to believe. Like Thomas we want personal revelation. In his rebuke of Thomas, Jesus tells us how important it is to have faith in him. He calls us to open our hearts and minds to the many ways in which he manifests his presence and his glory. He has given us the Scriptures and his sacraments to help us. He has given us the witness of many brothers and sisters who have experienced the risen Lord in their lives. We are called to be open to the Lord, both as receivers of his good news and as witnesses to others of our experiences with Jesus. We must remain strong in our faith, as well as strong in our witness of Christ. The power and majesty of our God are made abundantly clear to us if only we are open to him. Jesus calls "blessed" those of us who have not seen, and as our faith continues to grow he showers his graces upon us.

Were Not Our Hearts Burning!

(Matthew 1:18-25)

"For it is through the Holy Spirit that this child has been conceived in her."

Joseph had a tremendous faith in God, and was always open to the power of God's Spirit and the will of God for his life. Surely he was a holy man, and yet he had to be very confused by the amazing things that were going on around him. Yet, he continued to stay open to the Lord, and because he was open, the Lord was able to make known to him that all that was happening was according to his will. Joseph accepted the will of God, not fully aware of what was to come, but trusting that the Lord would provide. We are called to reflect on the faith and trust of Joseph. We are called to that same faith and trust when things in our own lives seem confusing or out of our control. So often we fail to trust the Lord in times of stress. We fall into the depths of fear and despair, and then are not open to the power and healing which the Lord desires to provide for us. Let us strive to emulate the faith and trust which Joseph showed. Let us always strive to stay open to the Lord amid all the stress of our trials and tribulations. Let us maintain our faith and trust in the Lord, no matter what is happening in our lives, knowing, as Joseph did, that God loves us and has promised to provide for us in all of our needs.

Blessed Are You Who Believe

(Acts 3:11-26)

"When Peter saw this, he addressed the people, 'You Israelites, why
are you amazed at this, and why do you look so intently at us as if
we had made him walk by our own power or piety?'"

The apostles had been preaching and healing people even before Jesus
ascended into heaven. Yet, there were many people who did not understand all that was happening, were still amazed when people were healed,
and were unable to comprehend the power and majesty of Jesus. St. Peter
wanted to be sure that the people knew it was the power of Jesus, which
was at work in the apostles. It was Jesus who was the Healer, and in the
power and majesty of the Lord, the faith of the people was able to be
built up, and many were added to the faith. The Lord continues to heal
and work many wonders in our lives and in our world. Like some of the
people listening to St. Peter, we, too, sometimes fail to understand all
that is happening in Jesus' name. Like some of those people, our faith
and confidence is sometimes disturbed by happenings in our lives and
in our world, even amid all that the Lord continues to accomplish and
the many times that he has acted in our lives. Other times, we look for
other explanations for the wonders our Lord performs. We are called to
be always aware of the living God, present and active in our lives and
in our world, as he continues to build our faith. Then we are called to
proclaim and share with others the goodness of God, as the apostles
did before us.

Were Not Our Hearts Burning!

(Mark 16:9-15)

"[But] later, as the eleven were at table, he appeared to them and rebuked them for their unbelief and hardness of heart because they had not believed those who saw him after he had been raised."

St. Mark goes out of his way to explain how hard it was for the apostles to believe that Jesus had been raised from the dead and had been seen, first by Mary and then by two more of the disciples. Each time someone had come forward to say that they had seen Jesus, St. Mark tells us that the apostles refused to believe. Finally, Jesus appeared to all of them and rebuked them for their unbelief. In speaking to the difficulty of the apostles' ability to believe what they had been unable to see for themselves, St. Mark is surely speaking to us. We are called to a high level of faith, a faith to believe something we have not seen. Although, we have not seen him with our eyes, Jesus helps us to believe by his powerful presence in our lives. He helps us to believe by the many gifts he continues to shower upon us, the most important being the gift of the Holy Spirit. And so, while we cannot see Jesus as did the apostles, through their witness and the many gifts which we are given, our spiritual eyes are wide open to the majesty and the glory of our risen Lord.

5

FAITHFUL IN HIS PROMISES

We live in the hope of God's promises. Our hope is well founded, because the Lord is eternally faithful in the promises he makes to us. He is the same yesterday, today, and forever. He will never forget the promises that he has made, and he will keep every one of them, in his time and in his way.

PRAYER

Most faithful God, keep us ever mindful of the promises that you have made, and of your faithfulness in keeping them. Bless us with the hope and courage to live always in the light of those promises.

Were Not Our Hearts Burning!

(1 John 2:24-29)

"And this is the promise that he made us: eternal life."

St. John reminds us that we have been given a promise by our God. He has given us the promise of eternal life. St. John tells us that it is this promise that compels us to follow the way of Christ. It is this promise that brings to mind all that we have been taught. We must never waver from what we know to be the truth. We must continually call on the Lord to strengthen our resolve to live in the light of the Lord, because we have everything for which to live. Jesus is our model. He taught us that there is nothing that can get in the way of our call to be reconciled to our Father in heaven. Everything that we must overcome, everything that we must endure on this earth is nothing as compared to the promise of eternal life. Jesus showed us that our God will turn every trial, every sorrow, and every suffering into joy, if we but persevere in our life of faith. The promise of eternal life, in the presence of our God, will sustain us, as long as we are mindful of that promise. We must never let the difficulty of our lives dim the promise of God. We pray that the promise of eternal life will strengthen and sustain us.

Faithful In His Promises

(Isaiah 2:1-5)

"O house of Jacob, come, let us walk in the light of the Lord!"

The prophet Isaiah begins to describe for us the change that will come with the coming of the Savior. He describes for us his vision, through the power of God's Spirit, of a world of peace. He describes a world in which there is no war, where people live in harmony under the kingship of Jesus. As we read this vision, and think about it in the light of the world in which we live, it may seem impossible to us. We see all of the turmoil, all of the division that is our world today. We see the rampant secularism in our own society, and wonder how this prophecy will be fulfilled for us. The Lord calls us to believe and to know that this and all prophesies that have been given to man through the power of God's Spirit are being fulfilled, and will continue to be fulfilled until every one has come to fruition. God's will for our world will be made manifest in his time. Our Lord calls us to live in the power of this prophecy. He calls us to begin to bring this Word, and his kingdom on earth, to fruition by the example of our lives. We are called to strive to conform our lives to Isaiah's vision for us. Let us pray for God's grace, that we may know his truth and live his vision for us, that our world may be transformed in peace and prosperity for all under the kingship of our Lord, Jesus.

Were Not Our Hearts Burning!

(John 8:51-59)

"Amen, amen, I say to you, whoever keeps my word will
never see death."

It is always important for us to keep our eyes firmly on our goal. Jesus has promised that for those who keep his commandments, the reward is life eternal. In this passage from the Gospel of St. John, he reminds us of that promise. He tells us that Abraham and all of those who kept the Word of God in their lives were glad to see the day of Jesus, because it was Jesus who conquered death and opened the gates of heaven to all believers. Jesus keeps his promises. He is forever faithful to his Word. That faithfulness gives us hope and builds our faith. That faithfulness helps us to stay focused on our goal. The trials and sorrows we face on earth, no matter how intense, are only temporary. They last only a short time in the context of eternity. The Lord calls us to rise above the trials we face now, and to look ahead to the glory that will be ours in heaven. He calls us to use the promise of that glory to help us on our way, to gain the strength to overcome our sinfulness, our trials, and our sorrows, and to follow more closely the way of the Lord. Our joy must be in Jesus, who, through his death and resurrection, has conquered death and given us hope of everlasting life with him in the presence of God, our Father, for all eternity.

Faithful In His Promises

(John 14:6-14)

"And whatever you ask in my name, I will do, so that the Father
may be glorified in the Son."

In this discourse, which Jesus directs to the apostles, he shares with us
the promise of his mission. He explains that he will return to the Father
to prepare a place for each of us. He reminds us that he is in the Father,
and the Father is in him. Jesus tells us that as we see and come to know
him, we will come to see and know the Father, because he is the face
and the perfect image of our God. Finally, he promises that when we
are one with him in our desire and in our prayer, he will do whatever
we ask in his name. Jesus certainly builds our hope in him, as our hope
is founded on all of these promises he has made and his faithfulness in
keeping them. The Lord calls on us to trust in him and the promises
that he has made. He calls on us to direct our thoughts and our actions
toward the fulfillment of his promises. It is when we direct our thoughts
and actions to the Lord's will for us, that we put on the mind of Christ
himself, and it is when we put on the mind of Christ that we will be
granted whatever we ask for in the name of Jesus, our Lord.

Were Not Our Hearts Burning!

(Deuteronomy 26:16-19)

"And today the Lord is making this agreement with you: you are to
be a people peculiarly his own, as he promised you; and provided you
keep all his commandments, he will then raise you high in praise and
renown and glory above all other nations he has made, and you will
be a people sacred to the Lord, your God, as he promised."

Moses reminds the people that they have made an agreement with the
Lord, and he has made one with them. As baptized Christians, we are
the descendants of this people of God, and the promises made to them
are the promises made to us. By virtue of our baptism, we have agreed
to follow the way of the Lord. We have agreed to forsake all other gods
and worship only the one true God. In turn, he has promised that when
we do follow his ways, we will be lifted up. We have even more than
the fulfillment of this promise to look forward to, because we are also
promised everlasting life in the new covenant, which our God has made
with us through Jesus. Let us be ever mindful of all of the promises of
the Lord. Let us live our lives ever in awe of the love God continues to
show us, and be always aware of the power we have in Jesus.

Faithful In His Promises

(Genesis 17:3-9, John 8:51-59)

"Jesus said to them, 'Amen, amen, I say to you, before Abraham
came to be, I AM.'"

Both of these passages remind us of the absolute and everlasting faithfulness of our God. We are reminded of the covenant the Lord made with Abraham, a covenant which promised that his descendants would be more numerous than the stars. We know that throughout our salvation history the Lord has improved on that covenant. We know that even as we, his people, have not been as faithful as we should to the covenants we have made with the Lord, he has always been faithful to his Word. As Christians today, we live under the new and final covenant that God has made with his people, sealed by the blood of his only begotten Son, Jesus. The life that we share in this new covenant, and the faithfulness of our God throughout our salvation history, enable us to have a certain hope that we will one day live with our God in heaven for all eternity. Our Lord has promised that he will raise up on the last day all who follow him and believe in him. Let us pray that we remain always aware of the blessings we receive under the new covenant with our God. Let us rejoice in the faithfulness of our God, and pray for the strength to be more faithful to our promise to worship him only, and to follow his teachings in our lives.

Were Not Our Hearts Burning!

(Isaiah 49:1-6, John 19:16-30)

"Though I thought I had toiled in vain, and for nothing, uselessly,
spent my strength, yet my reward is with the Lord, my recompense
is with my God."

Certainly it must have seemed to many that all Jesus had taught, all of the healings and miracles he had performed, were in vain. He had convinced many that he was indeed the Messiah, yet here he was hanging on the cross, crucified as a common criminal. After all that he had done, this looked to many like the end. Yet, they were to find out as we know, that it was only the beginning. The majesty and glory of God were made manifest in Jesus' death in a way no one would have ever been able to comprehend. Jesus was obedient and faithful to God's will, and in that obedience we have been saved. Many times it is hard for us to understand God's action in our lives. Many times it seems as if we toil in vain. We cannot understand how God could possibly turn what seems so impossible to us into something good. But he has told us that he can and will. He has told us that if we are faithful and obedient to his will for our lives, he will act. We may not understand it, but like Jesus, we must have faith in God's plan for our lives. He is our God, and he will make it happen!

Faithful In His Promises

(Acts 14:21-27, Revelation 21:1-5, John 13:31-35)

"He will wipe every tear from their eyes, and there shall be no more
death or mourning, wailing or pain, [for] the old order
has passed away."

As we read the promise of God in the book of Revelation, we are reminded
of the importance of keeping this promise always before us. We must
always keep it fresh in our minds, in the faith that our God has given
us, and in the certain hope that God will bring it to pass, because he is
faithful and true to his Word. As we travel on our life's journey, if we are
not grounded in the faith and hope of God's promises to us, it is easy
for us to become discouraged by the trials and sorrows of our lives. As
we become bogged down in the realities of this imperfect world, we can
easily become lost if we do not hold onto the promises of God. We can
easily see in the above passages that if it were not for the promises of
God, life would have become very difficult. From the knowledge of Jesus
that he would be betrayed by a friend, to the hard work of evangeliza-
tion that St. Paul faced, they were both able to face their trials because
of their faith and certain hope in the promises of God. We are called to
that same faith and hope as we strive to persevere in the trials that we
face every day, until all of our tears are wiped away and we live forever
in the presence of our God.

Were Not Our Hearts Burning!

(Luke 24:46-53)

"As he blessed them he parted from them and was taken
up to heaven."

As we read of the ascension of the Lord, it is a good time for us to reflect on our beliefs and the joy that we share in the many promises of Jesus. As we recall the events that led up to the ascension, we are called to remember that these events, the passion, death, and resurrection of Jesus, form the very essence of our faith. And as Jesus ascends into heaven, we recall his promise that he was to go back to his Father in heaven that he might intercede for us and prepare a special place for each of us. Jesus has certainly won the victory for us. He has conquered sin and death, and continually calls us to share in and live that victory in our lives. He calls us to live confidently in him, with the certain hope that as we persevere in striving to live good and holy lives, and that as we share in his victory here on earth, one day we will reign with him in heaven for all eternity. Let us join the apostles in praising Jesus and living joyfully in the glory of his light and love.

6

SAVED IN THE
BLOOD OF THE LAMB

Jesus is our Savior. He is our Redeemer. By his death and resurrection we have been saved. He has won the victory for us. He has reconciled us with our Father in heaven. With him, we are co-heirs of the kingdom of heaven, where he promises that those who believe will reign with him forever.

PRAYER

Our Lord and Savior, thank you for redeeming us. Thank you for reconciling us with our Father in heaven. Help us to live in the power of your death and resurrection, so that we might one day reign with you in your heavenly kingdom.

Were Not Our Hearts Burning!

(Jeremiah 31:31-34)

"I will place my law within them, and write it upon their hearts; I will be their God, and they shall be my people."

Through Jesus, our Father has made a new covenant with us. The Lord speaks of this new covenant through the prophet Jeremiah. He tells us that the new covenant will be one of love and faith. The Lord will place his laws and the knowledge of his love in our hearts. We will know him, not in the context of the law, but in the context of his love for us. He will plant in us the beautiful gifts of faith and hope. We know that the Lord has fulfilled this prophecy in Jesus. By the blood of Jesus we have been saved. We have been reconciled, in love, with the Father. In Jesus we see the love and the very face of God. In Jesus we experience the love that the Father has for each of us. In the person of Jesus we see the compassion and the power of God, as he heals and leads his people. Through the power and strength of Jesus, we are built up in our faith. We have hope that we will one day be raised up with him and live forever in the presence of the Father. We are blessed to live in the shadow of the new covenant that God has proclaimed in Jesus. Let us never forget how blessed we are. Let us never take for granted the love and power that God has given each of us through the new covenant he has proclaimed through his only begotten Son, our Lord Jesus Christ.

Saved In The Blood Of The Lamb

(John 6:35-40)

"And this is the will of the one who sent me, that I should not lose
anything of what he gave me, but that I should raise it [on]
the last day."

Jesus came into the world to save each one of us. There is not one of us
who is unimportant to the Lord. There is not one of us who is beyond
his saving power. Jesus loves each of us with a burning, unconditional
love. It may be hard for us to believe that the Lord could love each of
us so passionately that he would die for us, that the gates of heaven
might be opened for us. It may be hard for us to believe that, although
we stumble and fall so often in our lives, the Lord will never give up on
us, and will always forgive us when we confess our sins and rely on his
mercy in our lives. It may be hard to believe, but it is true. This passage
from John's Gospel is our certain hope that Jesus will never forget us. It
is a message of hope that the Lord will continue to forgive us and guide
us, no matter where we are at this moment on our journey of faith. We
must come to know and experience how blessed we are, and how loved
we are by our Father in heaven. We must come to know that it is his will
that not one of us should be lost, and that he sent his only Son that each
of us might be saved and made worthy by his sacrifice. The Lord calls
us to live in the light of this hope, to let this message of hope strengthen
us, give us dignity, and make known to us the depth of his love.

Were Not Our Hearts Burning!

(Hebrews 12:18-24)

Indeed so fearful was the spectacle that Moses said, 'I am terrified and trembling.'"

In Jesus we have a mediator between God and man. By his death we have been born into the family of God. In this passage from the book of Hebrews, we read of the contrast between the old and the new covenant. We come to understand how blessed we are to have Jesus as our Brother. Our forefathers knew God only through the prophets, and the other varied ways in which God chose to reveal himself. They had a very limited knowledge of God and lived their lives under the constraints of the law. In Jesus we see the face of God. We see clearly the love God has for his people. We see in Jesus how our Father delights in his children. With Jesus as our mediator, we have no fear of approaching our God, for we know that he cares for us. In Jesus, we have become his sons and daughters. We live our lives in the freedom of the Spirit, who has been sent to us as a gift from God. We live in the knowledge that we have been redeemed in the blood of Jesus. We are indeed blessed, and we are called to realize and live in the freedom and light of Jesus, who is our Savior and mediator. Let us praise and worship our God for the grace and mercy he has shown us in sending his Son to us, that we might come to know him and love him as he loves us.

Saved In The Blood Of The Lamb

(John 17:20-26)

"And I have given them the glory you gave me, so that they may
be one, as we are one, I in them and you in me, that they may be
brought to perfection as one, that the world may know that you sent
me, and that you loved them even as you love me."

In Jesus we have more than a friend, more than a brother. We have a
redeemer. We have an intercessor. Jesus has given us more than just life.
He has given us a part of his divine life. Through him, we share a divine
nature, as we have become a part of him. He is the head of the body, of
which we are members. In this passage Jesus gives us a glimpse of the
majesty, glory, and power that he means for us to share with him. We
get a glimpse of the tremendous love God has for us, and the dignity
he bestows on each of us in his Son Jesus. Jesus prays that we be one in
him; one in power, one in glory, one in love. That oneness, that power,
that glory, and that love come to us through God's gift of the Holy
Spirit. As we contemplate the life that Jesus has in mind for us, let us
open our hearts to the action of the Holy Spirit. Let us strive to reach
the perfection in holiness that Jesus prays we have. In Jesus we have so
much more than we can imagine. In Jesus we are so much more than we
realize. Thank you, Lord!

Were Not Our Hearts Burning!

(John 14:1-6)

"In my Father's house there are many dwelling places."

Jesus reminds us that he is with the Father, interceding for us and preparing a place for us. He reminds us of his love for us, and of the Father's desire that each of us claim the place Jesus is preparing for us. Jesus also reminds us that he is the Way. It is only through him that we can claim a place with the Father in heaven. As we reflect on the words of Jesus, we are called to keep our eye on the prize. The beauty of what Jesus has done, and is continuing to do for us, should keep us focused on our goal. We must make Jesus the number one priority in our lives. We must strive to follow all of his teachings and commandments. We must open our hearts and minds to his Word and his plan for our lives. As we come to understand that Jesus is the only Way for us, that Jesus is the only Truth for us, that Jesus is the only Life for us, we will begin to glory and rejoice in the path of the Lord. It will become less difficult for us when we come to realize the love with which Jesus guides us. The prize is a glorious one. Jesus calls us to keep our goal always before us to think of those things that are above, rather than those things of this earth.

Saved In The Blood Of The Lamb

(Hebrews 9:11-15, Mark 14:22-26)

"He said to them, 'This is my blood of the covenant, which will be shed for many.'"

As Jesus celebrated the Passover with his apostles, Jesus makes known to us the true love and blessing that his life on earth is to us. He confirms the will of the Father that he is giving up his body for us and for our sins. He makes known to us that he is offering his life for ours, that his blood is the blood of the new covenant, and as the author of Hebrews tells us, there will no longer be a need for any other sacrifice. This is the sacrifice that will be given for all people and for all time. To keep us ever mindful of this new covenant, to help us on our earthly journey, and to dwell in us thus making us a sacrifice to God, Jesus gives us the gift of himself, his own body and blood. What a marvelous gift! His precious body and blood unite us with him to the Father. They unite us in our belief of the divine Trinity. They unite us in love as brothers and sisters of Jesus, and sons and daughters of our Father in heaven. The establishment of the Eucharist, given to us as a gift from our Savior, sets us apart as co-heirs with him of the kingdom of heaven. Let us continually thank the Lord for the most precious gift of his body and blood, given to us as life-giving food, to nourish and strengthen us until he comes again in glory.

Were Not Our Hearts Burning!

(Isaiah 52:13–53:12)

"He grew up like a sapling before him, like a shoot from the parched earth; there was in him no stately bearing to make us look at him, nor appearance that would attract us to him. He was spurned and avoided by men, a man of suffering, accustomed to infirmity, one of those from whom men hide their faces, spurned, and we held him in no esteem."

Throughout his life Jesus was just an ordinary man. He had not come as a king. He had not come as an earthly leader. There was nothing special about his appearance or demeanor that would draw people to him. It was his message of God's love that attracted people. It was his kindness and compassion that brought people to him. Jesus was like each one of us in every way but sin. And so we are called to share God's love. We are called to be kind and compassionate as Jesus was, thereby leading others to see beyond appearances to the Truth that is Jesus. Our Lord died for our sins, and as we are ever mindful of his death, let us remember to never turn away from the mystery of the cross. Let us be always mindful of his most holy passion and the death that he suffered for our salvation. He died so that we might have life, and have it abundantly! Praise to our most holy Lord and Savior!

Saved In The Blood Of The Lamb

(Acts 10:34-43, John 20:1-9)

"We are witnesses of all that he did both in the country of the Jews and [in] Jerusalem."

The Lord is truly risen! Alleluia! In his death and resurrection, the victory has been won for us. In the passage from the Acts of the Apostles, St. Peter recounts all that Jesus did in his life and what has been accomplished in his death and resurrection. He reminds his hearers that the apostles have been eyewitnesses to all that Jesus did. In reminding his hearers, he also reminds us. He reminds us that what we read about the death and resurrection of the Lord in Scripture is not a story, not something that is symbolic, but is truly something that happened in history. And it is in the knowledge of Jesus' victory over death, that we, too, have won that victory. Just as St. Peter and the other apostles were witnesses to Jesus, we are called to that same task. We are called to be witnesses to the life that we have in Jesus. We are called to be witnesses to the love that we experience every day of our lives. We are called to be witnesses to the majesty and power of Jesus, which we see every day. We are called to be witnesses to the gifts our God continues to bestow upon his children, including the gift of the Holy Spirit, who teaches and guides us. Finally, we are called to build on the foundation of the apostles, with Jesus as the keystone, a holy sacrifice to God, as the victory of Jesus and the kingdom of God are made manifest on the earth.

7

Lord, Have Mercy

We live our lives by the mercy of God. Without the Lord's mercy in our lives, we would be lost. God's mercy allows us to seek forgiveness for our sins. Washed clean and freed from guilt, we are then able to continue to strive for the lives of holiness to which we are called by our most merciful God.

Prayer

Most merciful Lord, help us to always seek your mercy. Give us the courage to come humbly before you, acknowledge our sinfulness, always relying on your mercy to cleanse us and give us hope to begin again to follow you more closely.

Were Not Our Hearts Burning!

(Isaiah 43:18-25)

"Remember not the events of the past, the things of long ago
consider not; see I am doing something new!"

The Lord continues to call us to renewal. He continues to call us into his promise. He continues to call us into his love and joy. Our God is all knowing. He is all powerful. He knows that we have all done good and bad. He knows our strengths and our weaknesses. He loves us in spite of the many times we have failed to love him. We are all sinners. At one time or another, we have all turned our backs on the goodness and love of our God. The Lord calls us to sincerely confess to him all of our failings. He tells us that as we come to him, he will forgive us and welcome us back into his loving care. But he offers us even more. He offers renewal, a new beginning. He makes us worthy, through his mercy, and wipes the slate clean so we can begin again to live in the peace and joy of the Lord. He admonishes us that as we are forgiven, we must forget our past transgressions as he does. He reminds us that he has the power to change anything in our lives, to heal us, and to renew us in ways that seem impossible to us. But he says he will do it, and so he will do it. Let us open our hearts to the life-changing power of the mercy of God. Let us open our hearts to God's unconditional love. Let us be renewed, so that we may live in the love and joy of our Lord.

Lord, Have Mercy

(Luke 22:39–23:56)

"Just as he was saying this, the cock crowed, and the Lord turned
and looked at Peter; and Peter remembered the word of the Lord,
how he had said to him, 'Before the cock crows today, you will deny
me three times.'"

As we read the passion of the Lord, we are called to reflect on the suffering of Jesus and the reason he chose to endure this suffering. We are called to examine our own lives, so that we can more fully understand our own responsibility in the suffering and death of Jesus. We are called to reflect on the sorrow of the Lord as his apostles and disciples left him to suffer alone, going so far as to deny that they knew him. As the Lord looked over at St. Peter, we can only imagine the sorrow and loneliness that he felt. How many times have we denied Jesus by our words or actions? How many times have we turned our backs on the Lord because of our fear? These are all questions we must come to grips with as we reflect on the Paschal Mystery of Jesus. For it is in this mystery that we have been redeemed. It is in this mystery that we have been reconciled with God. It is in this mystery that our fear is forgiven and we are reunited in the love of God, as were St. Peter and all of the apostles and disciples who confessed their sins and believed in Jesus, our Savior.

Were Not Our Hearts Burning!

(Colossians 3:1-11)

"Put to death, then, the parts of you that are earthly: immorality,
impurity, passion, evil desire, and the greed that is idolatry."

Our Lord loves us just the way we are. We are his creation, formed in
his own image, and he delights in us. He loves us so much that he sent
his Son to die for our salvation. In Jesus we have new life. In Jesus we
have become sons and daughters of our Father. It is in this new life that
we rejoice. It is in this new life that we find our peace and joy. And so,
St. Paul tells us that we must forsake those things that keep us away
from the Lord. We must concentrate on those things that keep us close
to the new life we have in Christ. We are called to repent of our sins, to
turn totally away from their darkness. St. Paul calls to our minds several
of the sins that can be so difficult for us. These sins can be so difficult
because they are entwined in the lifestyles of our society. Our society
puts a premium on wealth and pleasure. St. Paul tells us that following
this way of the world will surely lead to our doom. Let us pray for the
grace to discard these ways of the world, and to instead base our lives
on the love and goodness of the Lord and those things that are above,
rather than the things of the earth.

Lord, Have Mercy

(Matthew 4:12-17)

"From that time on, Jesus began to preach and say, 'Repent, for the kingdom of heaven is at hand.'"

Jesus proclaims the kingdom of heaven through a call to repentance. He calls each of us to repent and turn away from sin and the ways of the world. He calls us to turn instead to the Lord. We cannot be a part of God's kingdom without repentance. Each of us has turned away from God by the many sins we have committed. Each of us is inclined to sin. The inclination to sin is part of our human condition. But God has given us the power to overcome our inclination to sin. He has given us the power to turn away from the temptations that plague our lives. He has given us his only Son, Jesus, to be our strength. He has given us the gift of the Holy Spirit to teach and guide us, and give us the knowledge and wisdom to follow the Lord in all of his ways. We know that it is never easy to conquer the temptations of this world, but God tells us that we must. We know that it is not easy to break the bad habits that we have learned and that have become a part of our lives, but God tells us that we must. Let us strive to heed the call of Jesus to repent. Let us strive to open our lives to the gifts of Jesus who strengthens us, and the Holy Spirit who teaches and guides us. Let us rejoice in the proclamation of the Lord, that the kingdom of heaven is at hand.

Were Not Our Hearts Burning!

(Genesis 4:1-15)

"If you do well, you can hold up your head; but if not, sin is a
demon lurking at the door: his urge is toward you, yet you
can be his master."

In this passage the Lord speaks to Cain about the human propensity
toward sin. He tells both Cain and us that we must always be on guard,
always ready to fend off the attack of the devil and evil in our lives. In
Cain, we have an example of how easily we can lose our way. We have an
example of how important it is to always do good and be vigilant against
the subtlety and trickery of the devil. The devil will use any weakness to
keep us away from the Lord. Our God tells us, however, that as difficult
as it can be to defeat sin and evil in our lives, we must never give up
hope. We have every tool we need to win any battle we face. We have
the tremendous gifts of God's grace and his all-encompassing forgiveness
and mercy. We have the life-altering gifts of the strength of Jesus, and
the knowledge and wisdom of the Holy Spirit. We have the example of
the saints, and all of the good men and women who have gone before
us; holy people who have shown us how to win the battle. All of these
gifts we have through the love and mercy of our God. As we are mindful
of all the good in our lives, and of all the grace and gifts of God, we gain
the strength and courage to hold our heads up, defeat evil, and attain
the reward of the just, an everlasting life with our God.

Lord, Have Mercy

(Luke 11:29-32)

"At the judgment the men of Nineveh will arise with this generation
and condemn it, because at the preaching of Jonah they repented,
and there is something greater than Jonah here."

The Lord continues to call us to repentance. He continues to put people into our lives to remind us of our call to holiness, to remind us that we have been created for something greater than a life on this earth. Jesus recalls for us the people of Nineveh who were living in sin. Our Lord sent Jonah to warn them of their impending doom. The people heeded Jonah and repented, coming back to the Lord, and in his mercy the Lord relented of his anger, and the people were saved. Jesus then reminds us that we have something far greater than Jonah in him. In the life and word of Jesus, we have something greater than we can imagine. In Jesus we have all that we need to change our lives and turn back to God. In the gift of Jesus, our God has given us the ultimate model for our lives. He has given us of himself that we might see his love, goodness, and mercy. We then have a responsibility to hear and follow Jesus, to repent of our sins, and to change our lives. Our God continues to call. Let us open our lives that we may hear, and then respond to his call.

Were Not Our Hearts Burning!

(Daniel 9:4-10, Luke 6:36-38)

"Be merciful, just as [also] your Father is merciful."

We know that we are sinners. We know that we have many times turned away from the light and love of the Lord. Too often, we have had to come before the Lord "shamefaced," as Daniel says, because we have failed to follow the Lord. We have asked our God to forgive us and shower his mercy upon us, and yet so often we fail to forgive ourselves. We find it hard to understand the depth of God's mercy. We find it hard to believe that God could continually forgive us, renew us, and take away our sin and our guilt. Jesus teaches us that the more we have mercy on others in our lives, the more we will come to understand God's mercy in our own lives. It is because Jesus has mercy on us that we can find the strength to have mercy on others, and it is in striving to forgive others in our lives that we begin to better understand God's divine mercy. As we come before the Lord, seeking his forgiveness and mercy in our lives, let us strive to forgive those who have wronged us. Let us make a sacrifice to the Lord by being merciful with others, as we are asking the Lord to be merciful to us. Let us share with others all that the Lord gives us, and thus help to bring to fruition the kingdom of God on earth.

Lord, Have Mercy

(Isaiah 1:16-20)

"Come now, let us set things right, says the Lord: though your sins
be like scarlet, they may become white as snow; though they be
crimson red, they may become white as wool."

God's mercy is boundless. It is unequivocal for those who come humbly
before him, confessing their sins and relying on his forgiveness. In this
passage, the prophet Isaiah prophesies in the name of the Lord. Through
Isaiah the Lord calls us back to himself, no matter what we have done
in the past, no matter where we are at this point in our lives. No matter
the situation in which we find ourselves, our Lord tells us that it can
be made right through his love and mercy for us. He tells us that all we
must do is turn away from the sin in our lives and embrace his truth.
All we must do is acknowledge our sinfulness, strive to do better, and
avoid the sins of our past so that we can live more fully in the light of
our God. We must remember that we are made worthy by our God. No
matter how we see ourselves, no matter how disgusted we are with our
past failures, no matter how far away from the Lord we find ourselves,
he, in his power and majesty, can and will change our circumstances.
He can and will heal us and bring us once again into full communion
with himself, bringing us his love, peace, and joy.

Were Not Our Hearts Burning!

(Micah 7:18-20)

"Who is there like you, the God who removes guilt and pardons sins
for the remnant of his inheritance; who does not persist in anger
forever, but delights rather in clemency, and will again have
compassion on us, treading underfoot our guilt?"

The Lord continually reminds us of his most gracious mercy. He continually reminds us that his mercy is always available to all who sincerely
strive to turn away from sin. The prophet Micah praises the Lord for
his mercy, restoring the lives of his people. The prayer of Micah should
be a prayer of hope for us. We know that we are a sinful people. We
know that many times we turned away from the Lord through sin. We
cannot help but feel guilty for turning our backs on the love and grace
of God. Yet here is Micah recounting the many times that the Lord has
removed the guilt of sin from his people. We are called to realize that
the Lord makes us worthy by his mercy in our lives. We are again called
to remember that the Lord "delights" to shower his mercy upon us, if
only we will turn to him. Let us keep before us the mercy that the Lord
has shown his people through all generations. Let us avail ourselves of
the most gracious mercy of God in our lives. Let us return to the Lord,
made whole and restored to life through his mercy.

Lord, Have Mercy

(Exodus 32:7-14)

"They have soon turned aside from the way I pointed out to them, making for themselves a molten calf and worshiping it, sacrificing to it and crying out, 'This is your god, O Israel, who brought you out of the land of Egypt!'"

Our Lord has given us as the greatest commandment to love him with all of our hearts. He has admonished us to put nothing in our lives before him. In our sinfulness, however, we often put other things in our lives ahead of our love for the Lord. God calls us to examine our lives and to make sure that we have our priorities straight. He calls us to love and honor him, and tells us that in that love and honor our lives will be complete. We are also called by God to pray for the people of the world. Many people in our own age become confused and turn away from the Lord, as did the Israelites. As Moses interceded with God on their behalf, we can intercede in prayer for all of the children of God on earth so that we all remain faithful to our God. We can pray that the Lord will come first in the lives of all people, because it is in following the way of the Lord that we find happiness and peace. It is in following the way of the Lord that we find salvation.

Were Not Our Hearts Burning!

(John 8:1-11)

"Then Jesus said, 'Neither do I condemn you. Go [and] from now on do not sin any more.'"

The Pharisees came to Jesus with a woman who had been caught in sin. They were ready to judge her according to the law. Jesus asked them if they themselves were without sin. They were forced to leave. Jesus sent the woman away with his blessing, and an admonition to sin no more. Like the Pharisees, we are often eager to judge the actions of others. We have little patience with people who have sinned, and we certainly see the wrong of it very clearly when it is someone else. Jesus calls us to remember that each one of us is a sinner. Each one of us has faults. Instead of judging each other, the Lord calls us to have forgiveness and compassion for each other. He calls us to pray for one another and to strengthen one another by example, compassion, and love. Certainly we are to speak out against sin as Jesus did, but we must realize that we are not the final judges of anyone. Only God knows the inner reaches of the heart. Only God is the judge of all peoples. Only he can judge in power and righteousness.

Lord, Have Mercy

(Genesis 50:15-26)

"Now that their father was dead, Joseph's brothers became fearful
and thought, 'Suppose Joseph has been nursing a grudge against us
and now plans to pay us back in full for all the wrong we did him.'"

Joseph had forgiven his brothers for the wrong that they had done him.
He told them many times that he had forgiven them, and yet, many more
times they were afraid that he would still hold a grudge against them,
and thus lived in fear that he would come against them. In our human
condition it is hard to believe that we can be truly forgiven for the sins
of our past, yet that is what the Lord does. We so often think in human
terms. In our society getting even and holding grudges are commonplace.
We may be, right now, holding a grudge against someone in our lives
making it impossible for us to think that God will forgive and forget the
many times we have sinned against him. Our God tells us that when
we sincerely confess our sins and vow to try harder to follow him, he
will indeed wipe our sins away. He tells us that not only are they wiped
away, but they are forgotten. He exhorts us to live our lives with hope
and courage, always looking forward, and not reliving our past mistakes
or living in fear of retribution for sins that have already been forgiven.
We are called to live in the grace and power of God's mercy, and then to
share that mercy with others in our lives.

Were Not Our Hearts Burning!

(Matthew 20:1-16)

"He said to one of them in reply, 'My friend, I am not cheating you.'"

In our human weakness we spend many of our waking hours comparing our lives with those around us. The devil is forever trying to promote jealousy in us. He is always striving to put in our minds the idea that we are not getting a fair break in relationship to others. He puts in our minds the idea that no matter what we have, we need more because others have more. Justice and equality take on a much more prominent role in our lives than they deserve. In this passage we see the effects of this type of jealousy. Even though some workers received all of the wages they had agreed upon, they were dismayed based on what others received. Their peace and happiness were destroyed because of a perceived injustice. The Lord calls us to concentrate on our own lives and to leave justice to him. He tells us not to lose focus on him, worrying about others having more. He calls us to trust him to provide all that we need. He calls us to trust in his perfect justice and to concentrate and strive for the goal of eternal life, which he promises all who follow his way. When we trust in the Lord, we will certainly be rewarded beyond our wildest dreams.

Lord, Have Mercy

(Ezra 9:5-9)

"I said, 'My God, I am too ashamed and confounded to raise my face
to you, O my God, for our wicked deeds are heaped up above our
heads and our guilt reaches up to heaven.'"

We are truly unworthy of the love and mercy of God. We all have sinned much, and have turned our backs on the goodness of the Lord. Some of us may even be away from the Lord at this very moment. It is when we have turned away from the Lord through sin, when we are distressed by the things that we have done to keep ourselves away from the Lord, that we must trust in his mercy. We must trust in his love for us. We must trust his Word that he can change our lives and our circumstances, that he can change our souls, turned scarlet through sin, snow white again. In this passage from the Book of Ezra, we find proof of exactly what the Lord has done for his people in every generation. He has promised that he will always be there for us when we turn back to him. And as we read this passage, we can see that he has kept that promise since the beginning of our salvation history. Let us turn back to the Lord. Let us rely on his mercy in our lives. Let us trust in his love for us, and live again, and always, in his wonderful light.

Were Not Our Hearts Burning!

(Haggai 1:1-8)

"Thus says the Lord of hosts: this people says: 'Not now has the time come to rebuild the house of the Lord.'"

In this passage the Lord is calling again for the people to change their lives. He calls for them to forsake their sinful ways and to turn back to him, to again follow his teachings and commandments. The people are sluggish and slow to change, but the Lord calls them to begin immediately. The Lord also calls us to change our lives. He calls us into a closer relationship with himself. He calls us to more closely follow his teachings and commandments. And he calls us to begin immediately, for like the Israelites, we can be sluggish and slow to start. So often we are comfortable where we are. We are comfortable that there will always be tomorrow. Our Lord tells us that the time must be now. He reminds us that we really only have this moment in time. We are guaranteed nothing more, and so he calls us to begin to change our lives today. He tells us that as we begin, he will be there to help us. He will give us the grace to succeed. He will touch our hearts anew and will send his Holy Spirit upon us. He will change our lives! Today is the day!

Lord, Have Mercy

(Joel 1:13–2:2)

"Yes, it is near, a day of darkness and of gloom, a day of clouds and somberness!"

Through the prophet Joel, our Lord warns those who have gone astray, those who have fallen away from him, those who have not heeded his call to return to him, that their lives will be filled with gloom and darkness. Just as the Lord spoke to the Israelites, he speaks to us. He reminds us that there will be a day of reckoning. He reminds us that he is the Judge of heaven and earth, and that each of us will be judged according to the way in which we have lived our lives on this earth. He warns that none will escape his judgment, and that those who have failed to seek his mercy in this life will have only darkness and gloom in the days to come. Just as there will be a time for judgment, there is a time for mercy. This is that time. This is the time to seek the forgiveness and mercy of the Lord. This is the time to return to the way of the Lord. This is the time to seek him out, to come into his love and his light and live in the joy; that is the way of the Lord. Let us pray that we will take full advantage of this time of God's mercy and grace, so that when our judgment day comes, we will be called to live in the presence of God forever.

Were Not Our Hearts Burning!

(Luke 15:1-10)

"I tell you, in just the same way there will be more joy in heaven
over one sinner who repents than over ninety-nine righteous people
who have no need of repentance."

We are all sinners. All of us have, at one time or another, found ourselves away from the Lord because of our sinfulness. As Jesus relates the story of the lost sheep, he gives all of us hope, for he tells us of his mercy and his concern for those who are away from him. Many people could not understand why Jesus would associate with sinners. They felt that Jesus should shun the sinner and only be with those who were blameless in the sight of God. Jesus responded that it was the sinner who truly needed him. This should fill us with hope and build our faith. In this lesson Jesus reminds us that he is with us always, that his mercy and compassion for all of us has no bounds and is never ending. In his love and mercy, Jesus claims us back. Let us pray to be ever mindful of the presence of Jesus in our lives. Let us pray to be always aware of Jesus' desire to claim us as his own. Let us always know that there is rejoicing in heaven as we all experience the love and mercy of God in our lives.

Lord, Have Mercy

(2 Samuel 12:1-12)

"The Lord sent Nathan to David, and when he came to him, he said: 'Judge this case for me!'"

In this passage David is forced to deal with something that plagues all of us. Nathan describes a sin to David. David becomes indignant and tells Nathan that in his estimation the sinner should be put to death for the severity of the crime. Then Nathan tells David that it is he, the king himself, who has committed the sin. Upon hearing this, David was astonished, but he took responsibility for his sin and confessed his sin to the Lord. Too often we are the same way. We can see the sin in others that we can never see in ourselves. We are quick to condemn others for the very same sins we ourselves commit. Like David, it is important that we recognize this fault in ourselves. It is important that we are open to the words of others in our communities so we can see ourselves in others' eyes. It is important that we take advantage of the grace and help the Lord provides in his sacraments. We are called also to follow the example of David in acknowledging our sins and in doing penance for our shortcomings. We must work through our sins with the Lord, as David did, and be reconciled with our God through his bountiful mercy. Our sins can weigh us down, but we must always remember that the mercy of God lifts us up, lifts us up into his glorious light. Let us praise the mercy of the Lord!

Were Not Our Hearts Burning!

(James 1:12-18)

"Blessed is the man who perseveres in temptation, for when he has been proved he will receive the crown of life that he promised to those who love him."

St. James reminds us that we will all be tempted. He reminds us that temptation will be a part of our lives on this earth and it will not end until we pass from this life to the next. He points out to us that temptation does not come from God, but from our own worldly desires. Temptation can end in sin when we give in to those desires. The grace of God can help us as we struggle with temptation. The Lord, in his love for us, will always help us to persevere if we but turn to him. He will protect us when we bring him into any situation that involves temptation. St. James uses the word "persevere" to remind us that the struggle against temptation will be a difficult one. He tells us however, that it is in perseverance we will be proved, and it is in being proved we will be rewarded with a crown of everlasting glory. So, let us not grow tired in our struggle with temptation, but let us stay well grounded in the Lord, praying constantly for his help and protection so that we can persevere against temptation and join him in heaven for all eternity.

Lord, Have Mercy

(Matthew 5:20-26)

"Therefore, if you bring your gift to the altar, and there recall that your brother has anything against you, leave your gift there at the altar, go first and be reconciled with your brother, and then come and offer your gift."

Our relationship with God is very much intertwined in our relationship with each other. Our Lord taught again and again that we must love each other, that we must forgive each other, and that we must have mercy on others as God has mercy on us. Our relationship with others is so important that Jesus teaches before we can be made worthy to offer a gift to him, we must be reconciled with our brothers and sisters. Jesus commands that we control our anger, comparing anger to the most grievous sins. It is always good for us to examine our lives, and to concentrate on the sometimes difficult command of the Lord to love more fully all of our brothers and sisters. It is always good for us to make a worthy effort to control our anger. Loving all people may sometimes seem impossible, but that is only an excuse. With God's grace, our lives can be changed. We are called to strive for holiness, as our God is holy. By his grace and our effort, we can make strides toward living the life to which we are called in Jesus.

Were Not Our Hearts Burning!

(Luke 15:11-32)

"Coming to his senses he thought, 'How many of my father's hired workers have more than enough food to eat, but here am I, dying from hunger.'"

In reading the parable of the lost son, we may sometimes find that we can see ourselves in his reluctance to return to his father. The son had asked for and been given his inheritance. He then left his family and squandered his inheritance. Now, in dire straits, his pride and shame is keeping him from returning to his father. He has been totally defeated and is ashamed of what has happened to him and the circumstances in which he currently finds himself. Finally, too hungry to worry about pride, he returns to a father who is overjoyed to see him, who forgives him and restores him to his place in the family. During our lifetimes, we may find ourselves in similar situations with our Lord. God, our Father, has given us the gift of salvation through Jesus. He has showered his love, mercy, and grace upon us; yet, we find ourselves far away from the Lord through our sinfulness. We may be far from him right now. We may be ashamed of how we have squandered all the gifts and blessings we have received from our Father, and so are afraid to return to him. We are called to follow the example of the lost son and put our shame and pride aside. We are called to return to our most gracious Father who is eager to forgive us and restore us to our place in the family of God. Let us pray for ourselves and for all who may be far away from the Lord, that we hear his call to return to him so we might receive his forgiveness and mercy.

Lord, Have Mercy

(Acts 9:1-20)

"Saul got up from the ground, but when he opened his eyes he could
see nothing; so they led him by the hand and brought him
to Damascus."

Saul had been persecuting the church with great vigor. He did not believe
that Jesus was the Messiah, and he was eager to arrest anyone who did.
On his way to Damascus in pursuit of Christians, Saul encountered Jesus
for the first time. He came to understand that he had been living a life
that was taking him away from God. He came to believe that Jesus was
indeed the Messiah. After this first encounter, as Saul arose, he found
that he could not see. It was not until after his baptism, when his sins
were forgiven through the mercy of God, that his sight was restored.
Like Saul, our own sin keeps us from clearly seeing Jesus. Because of the
blindness that comes from our sin, we may find ourselves further and
further away from the Lord. If we do not become aware and stay aware
of our sins, we cannot follow the way the Lord points out for us. Our
Lord calls us to be aware of the many times that we have sinned against
him. He calls us to come to him often so that we may confess our sins
and have our eyes opened in the power of his forgiveness and mercy.
With eyes wide open, we will be able to more closely follow the example
of St. Paul, in both living the Word of God in our lives and sharing with
others the goodness and love we experience in Jesus.

Were Not Our Hearts Burning!

(Mark 2:13-17)

"While he was at table in his house, many tax collectors and sinners sat with Jesus and his disciples; for there were many who followed him."

Jesus' promise of redemption is for every person. Every sin of every person was nailed to the cross of Jesus. His death conquered the sting of death for all people. In this passage Jesus called Levi, or Matthew, to be one of his disciples. He was to be one of the twelve, the closest followers of Jesus. This had to be very disturbing to everyone around Jesus, for Levi was a tax collector, and tax collectors were among the most hated people in Israel. And yet, Jesus brought Levi into his inner circle. He even dined with others who were sinners and tax collectors, as well as others who were the lowest of society. Jesus loved all of the children of the Father. He had come to proclaim the kingdom of God to all people. With Jesus it did not matter what a person was yesterday. Today was a new day, a day in which to repent and begin to live a different life, a life in the light and love of God. It is the same for us. Every day is a new day for us, because of the mercy of the Lord. Each day is a new opportunity for us to repent of our sins and to begin living the life in Christ to which we have been called. Our God is so good and so merciful to us. Let us proclaim his love and mercy and begin to live today the new life to which we are called in Jesus.

Lord, Have Mercy

(Luke 19:1-10)

"For the Son of Man has come to seek and to save what was lost."

In the Gospel story of Zacchaeus, Jesus teaches us one of the most basic truths of his mission. He tells us that he came to save sinners. He has come to save every sinner, losing nothing that the Father has given him, and bringing all sinners into the glory of God the Father. As Jesus was passing through his town, Zacchaeus was determined to see him. People who were considered followers of Jesus, tried to block him from seeing Jesus. They unintentionally got in the way of Jesus' stated mission of saving sinners. They first tried to keep Zacchaeus from seeing the Lord, and then grumbled about Jesus spending time with him. The Lord admonished them, and admonishes us, to make a path for all people who are seeking him. He calls us to help him in his work by being open to all who may seek the Lord. Like the followers of Jesus, we often think that we know who is worthy of Jesus' time, and who is not. When we think this way, we run the risk of getting in the way of the Lord's work. Let us reflect on our attitudes toward all those who are seeking Jesus in their lives and strive to be open to all. Let us pray that every person will come to seek the Lord, and that all of us remain open to the saving power of Jesus in our lives.

8

COME, FOLLOW ME

Our Lord calls each of us to follow him. He calls each of us into a closer relationship with himself. He has told us that he is the Way, the Truth, and the Life. In Jesus' life we have a model on which to base our own lives. In his commandments and teachings we are guided to be holy, as he is holy.

PRAYER

Lord, you call us to follow you. In your life, you have shown us the path we are to follow. You continue to guide us on our journey with you. Help us to see more clearly the path on which you lead us. Give us the strength and grace to follow your commandments and teachings, forsaking the way of the world and focusing more on you.

Were Not Our Hearts Burning!

(Luke 9:23-27)

"Then he said to all, 'If anyone wishes to come after me, he must deny himself and take up his cross daily and follow me.'"

We have often heard the saying, "Take one day at a time." That admonition is true in every area of our lives, including our spiritual lives. Jesus tells us that we must work daily in our efforts to follow him. We must make a commitment every day to take up our cross and follow the way of the Lord. We know that this will not be easy. The way of the Lord can be difficult for us. The world is constantly pulling us in a different direction. In addition, we have all been given different trials in our lives and different crosses to bear. With all that seems to be against our spiritual growth, we can become overwhelmed if we forget that Jesus is always with us showering his grace upon us. He calls us to come to him every day so he can assure us that with his love and grace we can overcome our trials, and more than that, live the life of a disciple of Jesus. Every time we pray the "Our Father," we ask the Lord to "give us this day our daily bread." As we pray the "Our Father," let us apply that request to both our physical and spiritual needs. Let this prayer be a reminder to us of Jesus' call to take up our cross and follow him. Let it be a prayer of faith and hope that the Lord will always supply the means for us to faithfully follow his way and to be his disciples.

Come, Follow Me

(John 8:31-42)

"Jesus then said to those Jews who believed in him, 'If you remain in my word, you will truly be my disciples, and you will know the truth, and the truth will set you free.'"

The Lord tells us again and again that it is his way, his teachings, and his commandments that are the design for our lives. The Lord reminds us that if we wish to follow him, we must remain in his Word. But, he tells us even more than that. He tells us that if we remain in his Word, we will know and understand the truth, and in that truth we will be set free. The Word of God is the power and the strength of our lives. His Word is the path by which we attain happiness and peace in this life, which is filled with trials and sorrow. Anything else to which we might cling may give temporary peace, but only the Word of God can give enduring peace, because it is eternal truth. We have been created to remain in the Word of God. Our souls long to remain in the Word of God. The Lord calls us to love and to cling to his Word. Let us always heed the voice of God. Let us remain strongly committed to follow the way of the Lord. Let us immerse our lives in his Word by listening, studying, and then living the Word, which God proclaims to his people.

Were Not Our Hearts Burning!

(Acts 18:9-18)

"One night in a vision the Lord said to Paul, 'Do not be afraid. Go on speaking, and do not be silent, for I am with you.'"

As St. Paul heard the call of Jesus to preach tthe gospel to the Gentiles, he relied on the promise of Jesus to be with him always. Our Lord told St. Paul not to be afraid. He gave St. Paul every gift that would be needed to carry out the mission to which he had been called. The Lord gave him courage and strength and often let St. Paul know that he was with him to guide and protect him. In our lives, as we strive to live out our faith, it is easy to become afraid. It is easy to become discouraged. We are constantly bombarded by the things of this world that so often fly in the face of the faith we practice. Oftentimes we must take positions that are contrary to the views of the majority. Our positions may even be contrary to those of family or friends. Yet, we must not falter. We must stay strong in our beliefs. Just as St. Paul needed the strength and assurance of the Lord, we know also that we cannot prevail on our own. We need the help and presence of the Lord, and must come to realize that just as the Lord was there for St. Paul, he is there for us. He will give us his strength and every other gift that we need so that we can boldly live out our faith. Our Lord will be with us always to guide and protect us. If we continue to be open to the Lord, we will hear his voice, as St. Paul did. We will hear him say to us, "Do not be afraid."

(Acts 20:17-27)

"And so I solemnly declare to you this day that I am not responsible for the blood of any of you, for I did not shrink from proclaiming to you the entire plan of God."

St. Paul took his call from the Lord very seriously. He knew that he had been given a task, and he worked day and night to perform that task to the best of his ability. We know that he endured many hardships and much suffering, and yet he did not stop doing the will of the Lord in his life. And as he tells us, he did not water down the teaching of the Lord to make it easier for those to whom he was preaching. We are called to take our faith just as seriously. We are called to make our faith the top priority in our lives. We are called to live our faith boldly and with courage. We are called to live our faith in its totality, not picking and choosing, and then discarding those teachings that may be hard for us. The way of the Lord is uncompromising. He wants all of us, all the time. We are his, and he claims us for himself. We know that through the trials and sufferings St. Paul was forced to endure, the Lord blessed him abundantly. Just so, the Lord will bless us when we take seriously our faith in him and live it boldly in his name.

Were Not Our Hearts Burning!

(John 21:20-25)

"What concern is it of yours? You follow me."

In this passage we find that St. Peter was concerned about how the Lord was going to treat one of the other disciples. He was concerned with whether everyone would be treated the same. This concern of equal treatment by the Lord can be one of the largest stumbling blocks in our walk of faith. In our lives, we are always interested with what is going on in our neighbors' lives. We are always concerned that we are treated as well as everyone else in every situation. We can easily lose focus of our goal if we concentrate our efforts on watching others. Jesus knows that this concern can be a temptation for us. Our Lord tells St. Peter, and us, that it is not our business to be concerned with the ease or difficulty of anyone else's life. He tells us that he has called us to follow him in all situations, and that we are called to concentrate our efforts on our goal to follow him. We must strive to stay on the path the Lord has pointed out for us. He admonishes us that it is he who will decide the fate of all people. It is to him only that all people belong. He tells us that if we concentrate on our own lives and our own call, our reward will be secured. The Lord has a plan for each one of us. It is a unique and wonderful plan. Let us strive to follow that plan, and not worry so much what is happening with others.

Come, Follow Me

(Matthew 8:18-22)

"But Jesus answered him, 'Follow me, and let the dead bury
their dead.'"

Jesus reminds us that we must be single-minded in our efforts to follow him. We must stay focused on him, despite all the temptations and distractions that befall us in our everyday lives. Our focus must be strong and unshakeable. It is so easy, with all that is going on in our lives, to become distracted. It can become easy to put the practice of our faith on the back burner as we attend to matters that can continually crop up in our lives. It can sometimes happen that our faith becomes neglected because other things of importance seem like they should be our top priority. Jesus tells us that there is nothing as important as following him. There is nothing more important than the development and practice of our faith. We are called to examine our lives to make sure that we are not confused about our priorities. We are called to pray for the grace and the wisdom to understand the importance of our faith in the context of the lives which we lead. Jesus must always remain our top priority. He must remain our all in all.

Were Not Our Hearts Burning!

(Luke 21:12-19)

"By your perseverance you will secure your lives."

Jesus reminds us that to follow him faithfully in our lives, we must have perseverance. He tells his followers that many of them will be imprisoned and others will suffer death. He tells them that nations will turn against each other, and even families will be torn apart because of decisions made to follow him. We see many of the things Jesus warned about happening in our world today. We see many Christian people suffering throughout the world for their decision to follow and proclaim the Lord. All of us can see the decline of religious virtues and belief systems in our societies. Many Christian ideals and beliefs are called reactionary, out of step, and even dangerous to a free society. Yet, Jesus says that he will never change. He tells us that we must stay faithful to what he has taught us and to stay always on the path on which he leads us. Let us pray for those who are being persecuted and are dying for their belief in the Lord. Let us all be aware of the constant battering of Christian ideals and virtues, which is happening all around the world. Let us listen to the voice of Jesus, as he encourages us to persevere and promises that all who do will receive a much greater reward in heaven.

Come, Follow Me

(Philippians 1:3-11)

"I am confident of this, that the one who began a good work in you will continue to complete it until the day of Christ Jesus."

St. Paul glories in the majesty and power of our God. He tells us of the desire of the Lord that we all one day live in his glorious presence forever. He exhorts us to say yes to the Lord. He exhorts us to remember all that we have heard and seen. He tells us of his own confidence, that in saying yes to the Lord we will be given every grace and blessing that we need to complete our journey with him. We have that same confidence, for we have seen that the Lord is always there for us when we invite him into our lives. He is there with his compassion in times of sorrow, with his grace in times of trial, and with his love that is always so powerfully present in our lives. When we invite the Lord into our hearts, our lives are filled with his power, they are filled with the gift of the Holy Spirit. Let us invite the Lord into our hearts. Let us say yes to him. Yes, Lord, we believe! Yes Lord, we need your grace, your mercy, and your love in our lives! Come, Lord Jesus, come!

Were Not Our Hearts Burning!

(Matthew 1:18-25)

"When Joseph awoke, he did as the angel of the Lord commanded
him and took his wife into his home."

Joseph was a man of uncompromising faith. He lived a holy life, always
open to the plan of the Lord for his life. Joseph heard the word of the
Lord and did not hesitate to follow his command. He followed the command
of God, even though it must have seemed impossible to his mind.
He was sure the Lord was speaking to him, and he opened his mind and
his heart to the word of the Lord. Would any of us have been as open as
Joseph? If we were in his place, could we be as faithful to God's word,
as improbable as it was? If we find ourselves slow to answer, we must
reflect on our relationship with the Lord. Joseph was able to positively act
on the word of God, because he was familiar with the voice of the Lord
in his life. He stayed close to the Lord, both in prayer and in the way he
lived so that he could be sure that it was the Lord speaking. Let us live
our lives in the faith of Joseph. Let us always stay close to the Lord in
prayer, as well as the way in which we live, so that we might always be
open to the voice of the Lord as he leads us and guides our lives.

Come, Follow Me

(1 John 2:1-11)

"The way we may be sure that we know him is to keep
his commandments."

St. John reminds us that there is more to being a Christian than just saying we are Christian. He tells us that we must walk the walk. We must live out our call from God. He teaches us that we walk the walk by following the commandments of the Lord. The commandments of God must be a guide for our lives. St. John says that it is incorrect to say we know God if we fail to follow his teachings in our lives. This may seem very elementary, but we must be constantly reminded that our actions speak louder than our words. It can be easy to find ourselves proclaiming we are Christians, while at the same time following the way of the world or picking and choosing which laws of God we want to follow. St. John calls us to reflect on our lives to be sure that we are following the commandments of God. He calls us to dedicate our whole lives to following the teachings of the Lord. He calls us to surrender our wills totally to the will of the Lord, and not to pick which parts of our wills we will surrender. Let us pray for the strength and grace to follow completely the laws of God. For St. John tells us that when we follow the commandments of God, we know him, and when we know him in our lives, we will have the peace and joy that only knowing him can provide.

Were Not Our Hearts Burning!

(1 Samuel 16:1-13)

"The Lord said to Samuel, 'How long will you grieve for Saul, whom
I have rejected as king of Israel?'"

Samuel had been by the side of Saul since the Lord had chosen him as
king of Israel. Because of his sinfulness, he was no longer favored by
the Lord. Our Lord's plan was to choose another king. Yet, Samuel's
heart had been closed to the Lord because he wanted Saul to remain
king. Finally, David is chosen, although Samuel, Jesse, and others had
thought that there were others of Jesse's sons who were more qualified.
Eventually we must come to realize, as Samuel did, that it is God's plan
for our lives and our world that is the most important. All of us have
strong ideas concerning the path our lives should take. God's lesson is
not that we shouldn't have these strong ideas, but that we should always
present them to him for his blessing. We are also called to be open to
the Lord if the path we have chosen is not his plan for our lives. We
must always be ready to follow the plan of our Lord, for he brings peace
and tranquility through his plan. He brings about his kingdom, which
benefits all. He brings about the fulfillment of his promise of everlasting
life where we will live in his presence forever.

Come, Follow Me

(Isaiah 42:1-7)

"Here is my servant whom I uphold, my chosen one with whom I am pleased, upon whom I have put my spirit; he shall bring forth justice to the nations, not crying out, not shouting, not making his voice heard in the street."

Our God tells us through the prophet Isaiah that he sent his Son, not shouting, not intimidating, not condemning, but by his spirit and love, changing hearts and bringing the kingdom of God to the world. We may sometimes wonder, as did the earliest followers of Jesus, why he was not more forceful in changing the world. We may wonder why Jesus did not just take over the world for God and conquer those who would not believe. It would have certainly made it easier for us. But our God has given us the gift of free will. He has given us this gift that he will never take away. He will never force us to do anything. Instead, he calls us to freely choose him and believe in him. He calls us to freely believe in his Son. He calls us to freely believe in the Holy Spirit. He calls us to freely choose his love over the uncertainty of our world, to freely choose his plan for our lives over the temptations of the world. Our God is gentle, always calling, always healing, always showering us with his love and grace. Let us open our hearts to him and freely choose to follow our most loving and gracious God.

Were Not Our Hearts Burning!

(John 21:15-19)

"Amen, amen, I say to you, when you were younger, you used to dress yourself and go where you wanted; but when you grow old, you will stretch out your hands, and someone else will dress you, and lead you where you do not want to go."

Jesus warned Peter that following him would not be easy. In fact, as this passage says, Jesus is telling Peter that he will one day die for his beliefs. When we make a commitment to follow the Lord, we will also find that many times our lives will not be our own. St. Paul told us that when we surrender our lives to the Lord, we live no longer for ourselves, but for him who died for our sins. He told us that our lives belong to God, both in life and death. St. Peter understood what the Lord was telling him, but did not back away from the commitment he had made, because he trusted that despite the sacrifices he would have to make, the rewards would be far greater. We are called to that same level of commitment. We are called to that same level of trust. We are called to surrender our lives to the Lord, to give our lives for the sake of his kingdom, and in that surrender find the peace and joy that St. Peter found in the Lord. As St. Peter surrendered his life to God, he was changed. We, too, can be changed into people who constantly live in the light and strength of the Lord.

Come, Follow Me

(Mark 5:1-20)

"As he was getting into the boat, the man who had been possessed pleaded to remain with him. But he would not permit him but told him instead, 'Go home to your family and announce to them all that the Lord in his pity has done for you.'"

In this passage Jesus cures a man who had been possessed by demons. After being cured, the man, in his gratitude, wants to stay with Jesus and become one of his disciples. But as we read, Jesus denied him his request. Instead he sends him home to his family to share with them the glorious things the Lord has done for him. We can certainly understand the man wanting to stay with Jesus, but Jesus had other plans for him. Jesus also has plans for each one of us. His plan is different for each of us and may not be the plan we would choose for ourselves. Regardless, we are called to discern and follow Jesus' plan. Each plan is important, each task is necessary, no matter how big or small. As St. Paul told us, some are called to be teachers, some prophets, some apostles, but each is called according to the same Spirit, and each is an important part of the whole. As we reflect on this passage, let us strive to wait on the Lord, to discern our role in his plan and to carry out his plan for our lives. For many of us as lay people, that task may start as it did for the man in this reading—sharing the goodness of the Lord with our families and modeling for them the love of our wonderful God.

Were Not Our Hearts Burning!

(Mark 8:27-33)

"You are thinking not as God does, but as human beings do."

As the Lord began to explain to the apostles that he was to suffer and die, it seemed very natural for St. Peter to protest. Yet, the Lord rebuked him for it, saying that St. Peter was speaking against the will of God for him. Any one of us might have protested, as did St. Peter. In the rebuke of the Lord, we see the lure of the world on all of us as human beings. We learn at the seemingly innocent tugging the world places on each of us as we try to follow the path of the Lord. We see that the way of the world and the way of the Lord can be very different. We learn from Jesus that we must continually be aware of the many things that try to lead us away from the will of God for our lives. Those temptations to abandon the will of God can come from anywhere. Just as was the case with Jesus, they can come from friends and family and can seem very subtle and innocent. That is why we are called to be constantly in prayer and communion with our Lord, always striving to discern his will for us. Just as Jesus lived in the power of the Father, we, too, are called to that same trust and life. We are called to place first in our lives all of the ways of the Lord. We are called to be steadfast, never wavering from our commitment to the will of God for our lives.

(Hebrews 4:14-16)

"For we do not have a high priest who is unable to sympathize with
our weaknesses, but one who has similarly been tested in every way,
yet without sin."

As we reflect on the death and resurrection of Jesus, we remember the suffering that he endured for our sake. We remember his holiness, as well as the call for us to live holy lives. We praise Jesus, who is our Lord and Savior, as we remember that he nailed our sins to the cross. But it is good for us to always remind ourselves that Jesus is also our Brother. He is our most holy example. He was a human being just like us, being tested in every way that we are tested. He knows every human emotion that we know. He has the same human feelings that we have. So, we know that we can always go to him for his help and consolation, no matter the situation we face. At the time of his suffering, in the throes of pain and agony, Jesus commended himself to the care of his Father. His faith in the love and goodness of God never faltered. He believed in the plan of God, even when it seemed that death would prevail. Jesus calls us to that same level of trust as we strive to discern the will of God for our lives. He calls us to turn our lives over to the love and goodness of our Father. He teaches by the example of his own life that as we trust our lives to God, our Father will be with us always, even in our darkest hours, and will bring good from the trials and sorrows in our lives.

Were Not Our Hearts Burning!

(Deuteronomy 6:4-9)

"Speak of them at home and abroad, whether you are busy
or at rest."

Moses reminds the Israelites that the Lord is God alone. He reminds them that it is their duty to love and serve the Lord, to praise and glorify his name, and to put him first in their lives. Finally, he reminds them that they have a duty to proclaim his name in everything they do. In speaking to the Israelites, Moses speaks to us also. The obligation and duty of the Israelites to love, serve, and proclaim the Lord on earth has now fallen to us. We are called to put God first in our lives. We are called to reflect on our lifestyles to make certain that we are following this command of God. We are called to love and serve him. This involves giving the Lord of our time, talent, and wealth. Again, we must reflect on our lifestyles to make sure that we are following this admonition. Finally, we, too, are called to proclaim his majesty and glory. We are called to proclaim him both in word and action. It is important that people know we are Christians. It is important for people to know that we know and experience the love of God in our lives. It is important for our own lives, too, that we proclaim God both in word and action, so that our own faith and trust are built up, and as we are strengthened, we come closer to the Lord, our God.

Come, Follow Me

(Matthew 18:1-5)

Whoever humbles himself like this child is the greatest in the kingdom of heaven."

To conform our wills to the plan of God for us can be a very difficult thing to do. From the earliest days of our childhood, we have been prepared to be self-sufficient. We have been taught to look out for ourselves and to promote ourselves. We have been groomed to "grow up" from the time we were little children. Yet, here is Jesus telling us that we must become like little children to enter the kingdom of heaven. It is difficult for us to give up our freedom to turn our lives over to anyone, even the Lord, but this is what he commands. He calls us to place our lives into his hands. He asks that we trust him in all that we do. He asks us to obey his commandments. He asks us to follow his path. Let us pray that we might become as trusting and compliant as children in our relationship with our Lord. Let us pray for a new and strong gift of humility, that we might hear our Lord more clearly and then follow him more closely. Let us pray that we receive the grace to realize that God knows what is best for our lives, and that he wants only good for us. Finally, let us pray that in trusting the Lord more fully and following him more closely, we come to enjoy the happiness and peace in our lives, which only the Lord can provide.

Were Not Our Hearts Burning!

(Matthew 23:1-12)

"For they preach but they do not practice."

Jesus reminds us that he has raised up shepherds to lead us. He reminds us that they have authority in him. As the sheep of his flock, Jesus calls us to practice that which his shepherds teach in his name. He reminds us, too, that those shepherds, just like all of us, are human, and as human beings are prone to weakness. Jesus uses the example of the scribes and Pharisees. He tells us that even as they sit on the seat of Moses and have that authority, they do not always practice what they preach. They do not always follow the same laws to which others are called to be obedient. In this example, our Lord makes known to us that there will always be a few shepherds who behave like the scribes and Pharisees about whom he speaks in this passage, just as there are those of us who sometimes find it difficult to practice that which we preach. There are times when scandal is caused and people turn away from the Lord. Jesus reminds us that to turn away from him because of the failings of others is not the way for us. He reminds us that it is he who is our one true Shepherd. He calls us to stay focused on him. If we do stay focused on him, we will never be disappointed. He will never let us down in the way our fellow human beings are capable of letting us down. He will always be the same. He will always be faithful to his love for us. So, let us follow Jesus. And let us pray for those shepherds and other Christian people who preach the way of the Lord, but do not follow that way in their lives.

Come, Follow Me

(Luke 6:1-11)

"Some Pharisees said, 'Why are you doing what is unlawful on
the sabbath?'"

Throughout his life on earth, Jesus said that he did not come to abolish
the law. He told us time and time again that he came to make clear the
laws and the way of God. The Pharisees were sticklers for the law, but
they often followed the law for the law's sake. Jesus has told us that it is
God's desire that we follow his laws in order that we might come closer
to him. In following his laws, we come to know the mind of God. We
come to know his plan for our lives. We find true happiness and peace.
If we do not try to understand and experience the love of God in our
lives, we run the risk that we will end up following the law only for the
law's sake. If we do not open our hearts to the teaching and guidance
of the Holy Spirit, we can become dead inside, as did a number of the
Pharisees. We, too, could lose all focus on what is truly important on
our journey with the Lord. Let us pray that we are always open to the
power of the Holy Spirit in our lives, that our faith will grow and mature,
and that we always have a strong, living faith. Let us pray that we never
get so caught up in the letter of the law that we forget about the spirit
of the law, and remember that the laws of God are always designed to
bring us closer to him.

9

COME, HOLY SPIRIT

Our Lord has given us a powerful gift in the Holy Spirit. He has promised that the Holy Spirit will guide us, teach us, reveal God's truth, and be with us until Jesus comes again in glory. When we open our hearts to the Holy Spirit, we become a temple in which he lives, bringing with him gifts, fruits, and virtues that help us on our journey. We have life in the power of the Holy Spirit. We have strength in the power of the Holy Spirit. We experience the love of God in the power of the Holy Spirit.

PRAYER

All-powerful Father, send the gift of your Holy Spirit upon us. Open our hearts to all that you have promised through the gift of your Holy Spirit. Holy Spirit, come into our hearts. Guide us. Teach us. Convict our hearts in God's truth. Come with your fire to change us. Live in our hearts and supply us with your fruits and virtues for our own spiritual growth, and with your gifts, that through us the kingdom of God may grow in our world.

Were Not Our Hearts Burning!

(Acts 2:1-11, 1 Corinthians 12:1-11)

"To each individual the manifestation of the Spirit is given for
some benefit."

Jesus has told us that he will be with us until he comes again in glory.
He will be with us to teach, guide, and build us into a pleasing sacrifice
to God the Father. When Jesus ascended to sit at the right hand of the
Father, he sent, as he had promised, the gift of the Holy Spirit upon
his apostles and disciples. The Holy Spirit came as tongues of fire. The
apostles and disciples of the Lord were changed by the power of the
Spirit, and through that power they were strengthened, and through
them many were added to the faith. The Holy Spirit continues to come
upon all of us who believe and desire him in our lives. He continues to
come as fire upon us to strengthen us, and through his power in us to
add many to the faith. The Holy Spirit works in every one of us who
believe, just as he worked in the apostles and the saints who have gone
before us. He continues to build up the church through the many gifts
that he bestows upon those who are open to him. Let us open our hearts
to him. Let us open our lives to his power, his truth, and his guidance in
our lives. Let us open our lives to the many gifts which he brings each
of us, so that our faith might continue to be strong, continue to be a
beacon in the darkness, continue to be a sign of hope, and continue to
be a sacrifice of praise to God the Father.

Come, Holy Spirit

(Acts 9:1-20)

"Immediately things like scales fell from his eyes and he regained his sight."

The conversion story of St. Paul is an example of the power of the Holy Spirit that brings power to our own lives. St. Luke tells us that when the Lord came in power to St. Paul, he was thrown to the ground. In rising to his feet, he was unable to see. It was not until Ananias, by the power of the Holy Spirit, touched his eyes that he was able to see again. He was immediately baptized and received new life and an infusion of the Holy Spirit, who was to guide him for the rest of his life. Many times in our own lives we are blinded to the ways in which the Lord leads us. We are not open to his voice in our lives. We are content in our darkness. Just as he infused St. Paul with the gift of the Holy Spirit, our Lord longs that we be open to the power of the Holy Spirit in our lives. If we have been baptized, we have already been sealed with the Holy Spirit. The power of the Holy Spirit is in us, ready to open our eyes to newness of life in Christ. Just as St. Paul's life was changed by the power of the Holy Spirit in his life to a new way, a way of new joy in the teachings of Jesus, so our eyes will be opened by that same Holy Spirit. We have been born again in Christ and given the power of the Holy Spirit. Let us open our lives to that power that our eyes may be opened to newness of life in Christ.

Were Not Our Hearts Burning!

(Numbers 11:25-29, Mark 9:38-41)

"Would that the Lord might bestow his Spirit on them all!"

In both of these passages some of the followers of the Lord are disturbed because there are others besides them who are filled with the Spirit of God, and therefore are able to do the works of the Lord. In the passage from the Gospel of St. Mark, our Lord tells his disciples not to prevent others from doing his work because the works are indeed from him. Moses tells his followers that it would be wonderful if all were given of the Spirit. What Moses hoped for has become a reality for us. Our God has sent the gift of the Holy Spirit to fill the earth. He has sent the Holy Spirit to renew the earth. He has sent the Holy Spirit to dwell in the hearts of all who desire him. We are filled with the Holy Spirit through the sacraments of baptism and confirmation. If Moses were here today he would hope that all of the people would come to know that the Lord has bestowed his Holy Spirit on them all! The Lord has given us the gift of the Holy Spirit. Let us open our hearts to his power. Let us open our hearts to his guidance. Let us open our hearts to him that we might do the mighty works of the Lord. Let us open our hearts to him that we might be renewed and the kingdom of God established on earth.

Come, Holy Spirit

(Romans 8:12-17)

"For those who are led by the Spirit of God are children of God. For you did not receive a spirit of slavery to fall back into fear, but you received a spirit of adoption, through which we cry, Abba, Father!"

The gift of the Holy Spirit, which we have received, is a Spirit of freedom. There are times in our lives when we may feel burdened in our faith by some of the more difficult commandments and teachings of the Lord. The secular world in which we live can make it more difficult for us to follow the way of the Lord. We can really feel the pull between the way of God and the way of the world. St. Paul exhorts us to never forget the power we have in the Holy Spirit. He calls us to be constantly aware of this most precious of gifts, especially when our lives become difficult. It is through the power of the Spirit in our lives that we are able to overcome all of the obstacles we face. But, St. Paul tells us even more. He tells us that it is only by the power of the Holy Spirit in our lives that we have true freedom. It is only in the power of the Spirit that we come to know that we are the beloved children of God. It is only in the power of the Spirit that we have the confidence to call God, "Abba" Father. Let us claim the power and the joy that God promises through his gift of the Holy Spirit. Let us be truly free in the Holy Spirit, our Father's glorious gift to his children.

Were Not Our Hearts Burning!

(Luke 10:21-24)

"In that very moment he rejoiced [in] the Holy Spirit and said, 'I give you praise, Father, Lord of heaven and earth, for although you have hidden these things from the wise and the learned you have revealed them to the childlike.'"

Jesus' entire life was spent in openness to the prompting of the Holy Spirit. In that openness to the Spirit, he was always living in the will of the Father. He was always aware of God's plan for his life and his plan for establishing his kingdom on earth. Jesus is a true example for us of always being open in prayer to the power of the Holy Spirit. He calls us to follow his example, always open and always living in the power the Holy Spirit will bring to our lives. As we strive to come closer to the Lord, as we strive to lead holy Christian lives, Jesus calls us to rely on the Holy Spirit, and through the power of the Spirit surrender our lives to him. He calls us to rejoice always in the plan of the Lord for our lives, as revealed through our openness to the Spirit. If we will prayerfully wait on the Lord in the power of the Spirit, he will make his way known to us. He will use us in spreading his love among the people. He will use us as he continues to establish his kingdom on earth. Come, Holy Spirit, come!

Come, Holy Spirit

(1 John 3:22–4:16)

"Those who keep his commandments remain in him, and he in
them, and the way we know that he remains in us is from the Spirit
that he gave us."

Through the precious gift of the Holy Spirit, we receive virtues, fruits,
and gifts, which give us strength to persevere in our call to be holy and
faithful Christians. We receive guidance and insight that help us on the
journey we travel in this world. The gift of the Holy Spirit could not be
more important. Jesus has told us that we will understand all through the
Advocate whom the Father would send. St. John confirms that it is in the
power of the Spirit whom the Father gave us that we truly know that God
remains with us as we strive to follow the way of the Lord. All of us have
questions and concerns about how we are called by God, about what we
are called to do on this earth, so that we may attain our goal of heaven.
All of us want to be reassured that we are living good Christian lives, the
lives to which we are called in Jesus. St. John tells us that our questions
will be answered and we will be reassured as we open our lives to all that
the Holy Spirit longs to give us. The Holy Spirit is so important to our
lives with all of the gifts he showers upon those who are open to him.
Our Lord exhorts us to never let this gift of the Spirit lie dormant in our
lives, but to live in the Spirit as we struggle through this life on our way to
everlasting life in heaven.

Were Not Our Hearts Burning!

(John 3:22-30)
"So this joy of mine has been made complete. He must increase; I must decrease."

It is hard for us to imagine the great humility of John the Baptist. Here was a man who had become famous throughout the land. He was much sought after as a teacher and healer. He had led many to repent and had baptized multitudes of people; now, as Jesus was beginning his public ministry, he was being asked by God to step away. We can only imagine how hard that would be for any of us. We have only to examine the feelings we would have if we were in the limelight and were then asked to step away and make room for someone else. It would be very difficult for us, as it would have been for John the Baptist, except that St. John was filled with the power, the wisdom, and the understanding of the Holy Spirit. By the power of the Spirit he understood his ministry. Because he was so blessed, he was able to proclaim the glory of the Lord Jesus, and at the same time fade into the background in complete joy and peace. It is to that confidence and that life in the Spirit to which we are called. It is to that level of wisdom and understanding to which we aspire. Let us pray for a new outpouring of the Holy Spirit in our lives. Let us pray for a new gift of humility and for the wisdom and understanding of the Spirit that we may live our lives in the peace and joy these gifts bring. Let us pray that we are always aware Jesus must always be first, and that as he increases in our lives, we will live more fully in his light and his love.

Come, Holy Spirit

(Luke 4:1-13)

"Filled with the Holy Spirit, Jesus returned from the Jordan and was
led by the Spirit into the desert for forty days, to be tempted
by the devil."

In this passage we read that indeed Jesus was like us in every way. Just as we are constantly tempted in our lives, Jesus was tempted by the devil. The devil used everything he could against Jesus. He used every trick and played to every feeling and emotion that Jesus had. It was only by the strength he received in the Spirit in his baptism and his faith in the love and help of the Father that helped him stay strong in the hour of his temptation. His grounding in his faith was a rock to him as he faced the wiles of the devil. In our lives we face temptations every day. The devil uses everything he can against us. Like Jesus, we must use every power that we have in our faith to resist the devil. Like Jesus, we have been given the gift of the Holy Spirit, by virtue of the sacraments of baptism and confirmation. We must learn to live in and use the power of the Holy Spirit we have been given. Our God has told us that he is our strength, and like Jesus, we must rely on his love and help in times of temptation. Finally, we must be always grounded in our faith. We must live it every day, so that when temptation comes we will have our faith to fall back on for strength and comfort. Let us thank the Lord for the gifts of his Son and of the Holy Spirit who live within us and stand beside us as we wage war with the devil.

Were Not Our Hearts Burning!

(Acts 2:36-41)

"Now when they heard this, they were cut to the heart, and they
asked Peter and the other apostles, 'What are we to do,
my brothers?'"

St. Peter's words on Pentecost had a powerful effect on many of the
people who were listening. Through the power of the Holy Spirit, not
only was St. Peter empowered to speak more forcefully than ever before,
but also the ears of those who were listening were open to the words he
spoke. Their hearts were convicted that indeed Jesus was the Messiah.
Many of the people were now coming to the apostles for instruction on
what they were to do. There are many voices in our own lives, voices
calling us to change our lives or stay the course in our faith, trying to
lead us on the path to which the Lord has called us. Our pastors, sacred
Scripture, and our communities are only a few of the voices that call us
to come closer to the Lord. We are called to open our hearts to the power
of the Holy Spirit, that as we hear these voices, we listen, and that as we
hear these voices calling to us, we respond in the positive way the Lord
desires. Then as we share the Good News of the gospel with others, we
are called to listen in the power of the Holy Spirit, as did St. Peter and
the apostles, so that we are better able to help others as they struggle
with the changes that come when hearts are first opened to the Lord in
a new way. Come, Holy Spirit! Help us to better hear and listen, both to
the call of the Lord and to the words of others in our lives.

Come, Holy Spirit

(Acts 4:13-21)

"Observing the boldness of Peter and John and perceiving them to
be uneducated, ordinary men, they were amazed, and they
recognized them as the companions of Jesus."

After Pentecost the apostles were changed. The Jewish officials recognized them as companions of Jesus, but where they had in the past been ordinary followers, they were now bold leaders. Because they were open to the power of the Holy Spirit, God was able to use them and mold them into the powerful tools for Christ that they became. It is inspiring for us to see that they were indeed just ordinary men. They were not special in themselves, but were made worthy in Jesus through the power of the Holy Spirit. They only had to be open to him and then work with the gifts and graces he provided. We may know people in our own lives who seem to be able to do more and work beyond their limitations and endurance, yet, we may think that we could never do the same. In the Acts of the Apostles, however, we read of people, ordinary in every way, doing mighty works for the Lord. We are called to be a part of that legacy through our openness to the Holy Spirit. The Lord continues to perform mighty works through ordinary people who are open to the Holy Spirit. Let us open our hearts and lives to him. Come, Holy Spirit!

Were Not Our Hearts Burning!

(Acts 4:23-31)

"As they prayed, the place where they were gathered shook, and they were all filled with the Holy Spirit and continued to speak the Word of God with boldness."

The disciples of the Lord faced many obstacles in their mission to bring the good news of the gospel to the people of the world. Their walk in the power of the Holy Spirit was an ongoing journey. They continued to pray for and receive the gifts and the power of the Holy Spirit. They continued to need renewal in the power that they had received. They continued to need more strength and courage as they continued to preach, teach, and heal. Throughout the book of the Acts of the Apostles, we read of new outpourings of the Holy Spirit upon the disciples. We, too, need renewal in the Spirit. We continue to need his strength and courage in our lives. Our lives as Christians today are surely as difficult as the lives of the disciples of the early church. So, we can expect that when we pray, we will be given all we need to help us live and share the good news of the Lord. A life in the Holy Spirit demands continual attention and prayer, for if we are constant in seeking him and the gifts he brings, he will be faithful in providing all that we need.

Come, Holy Spirit

(John 14:21-26)

"The Advocate, the Holy Spirit that the Father will send in my
name–he will teach you everything and remind you of all that [I]
told you."

As we read and study the Gospels of the New Testament, we become
aware that the apostles were never quite sure of all that Jesus told them
concerning his teachings and commandments. What Jesus was teaching
flew in the face of many of the things the people believed strongly in
and held dear. Their faith, as well as their culture, was longstanding and
deeply ingrained in the people. So, when Jesus came with his message,
there was inevitably confusion and many questions. While Jesus was with
them he taught and explained all that he could, but told the apostles
that there would still be questions when he ascended into heaven. He
told them that the Father would send the gift of the Holy Spirit to teach
them and to remind them of the way of the Lord. We certainly need that
same gift of the Spirit in our world. There are still many questions, many
conflicts between our faith and our society, so much left to learn. Our
Lord reminds us that the gift of the Holy Spirit promised to the apostles
is also promised to us. Let us open our hearts to this magnificent gift.
Let us open our lives to the teaching and guidance of the Holy Spirit as
we strive to discern and follow the way of the Lord.

Were Not Our Hearts Burning!

(1 Thessalonians 5:16-24)

"Do not quench the Spirit."

Jesus is the fulfillment of all God's promises. In him we have life. The Father sent us the gift of the Holy Spirit in the name of Jesus so that we are always aware and able to experience Jesus in our lives. It is by the power of the Holy Spirit that we are able to live bold Christian lives. St. Paul reminds us that we must never quench the Holy Spirit in our lives. In all circumstances, in all of our trials, in all of our suffering, we must allow the power of the Spirit to work in us. If we quench the Holy Spirit, if we let the flood of trials and sufferings douse this precious gift of God, we will surely be lost. We know that in times of suffering and difficulty it is so important for us to know that the Lord is with us, that he cares about what happens to us. This is exactly what we know through the power of God's gift of the Spirit. Let us pray for a new outpouring of the Holy Spirit. Let us resolve to never quench the Holy Spirit in our lives, but to always live in the knowledge of this most precious gift of God as we walk in his strength and his light.

I WILL GIVE YOU REST

Our lives are filled with temptations, trials, and sorrows. In this imperfect world this will always be true. Our Lord wants us to know, however, that he will always be with us. He will always be there to help carry our load. In his great compassion for us, he will always be there to lift us up.

PRAYER

Most compassionate Jesus, make us always aware of your loving presence in the sorrowful times of our lives. Help us in our trials, and keep us safe in times of temptation. Help us to understand that there will always be hardship, but that in that hardship, you are always there to help, comfort, and protect us.

Were Not Our Hearts Burning!

(Lamentations 2:10-22)

"Worn out from weeping are my eyes, within me all is in ferment;
my gall is poured out on the ground because of the downfall of the
daughter of my people, as child and infant faint away in the open
spaces of the town."

The temple had been destroyed. Israel had been conquered. The people
were in despair, questioning why God had brought this about, wonder-
ing if they would ever be restored. There are times in our lives when we
could read this passage and note that it reflects our own lives. Sometimes
in our lives we feel vanquished. We lose hope. We wonder why this
trial or suffering has been inflicted upon us. We wonder if we will ever
be delivered and restored by our God. There seems to be nothing but
sorrow for us. It seems as if it will go on forever. These times, when our
hearts are so closed, are the times we must rely on our faith and trust in
the Lord. These are the times that we must continue to try to open our
hearts to the compassion and comfort of our most loving God. The sorrow
may last for a while, but in the care of our most compassionate God, we
will find refuge, and through our faith and trust, the Lord will one day
restore us into the bright light of his peace and joy. We must never give
up on the Lord's love for us, because he will never give up on us.

I Will Give You Rest

(Mark 6:45-52)

"He got into the boat with them and the wind died down."

Our lives can be compared to being a boat in a storm. We are tossed about by the trials and temptations of this world. We are buffeted by the constant attempt of the devil to lead us into darkness. We become distraught in the sorrows that come into our lives. We are afraid, because it seems as if the storm will rage on forever. Many times it feels as if the boat, which is our life, is about to flip over or sink. We can easily reach the point of hopelessness and despair if we allow the storm to rule us. In this passage we read of the apostles' fear as a storm raged around them. It was only when Jesus came to them across the water, and they realized that it was he who was with them, that the storm subsided. We are called to be mindful of the fact that Jesus is with us. We are called to be mindful of the strength and power we have in Jesus. We are also called to be mindful of our own weakness and dependence on the Lord. It is only in Jesus that we find true peace in the storms of this life. We always have him with us if we follow the way in which he leads us. We always have him with us in Scripture and sacrament. We always have him with us in the compassion of our communities. We never have to be fearful of being alone or overpowered by the storm. We always have Jesus!

Were Not Our Hearts Burning!

(Mark 1:40-45)

"Moved with pity, he stretched out his hand, touched him, and said to him, 'I do will it.'"

Our Lord wants what is good for us. He longs to heal us in every way that we need to be healed. He longs for us to come to him in our sorrow and in our need for healing so that he can touch our lives and heal us. St. Mark tells us of a leper who approached Jesus, acknowledged his own weakness, and asked the Lord to help him. The Lord was filled with pity for this unfortunate man. The leper showed his faith by proclaiming the power of Jesus. Jesus responded to that faith by healing the man. Our Lord calls us to come to him. He calls us to acknowledge our weakness and our need for him. He tells us that when we come to him in humility and faith, he will always be there to comfort, help, and heal us. He loves us and feels the utmost empathy with the trials and sorrows of our lives. He wants us to know that we can and should always come to him in our sorrow and need. Let us pray for the humility and faith to come always before the Lord in our need. Let us pray for the ability to receive and experience the compassion and the healing of the Lord in our lives. Let us pray to be always aware that we are not alone in any struggle or circumstance, and that the Lord is with us, guiding our lives and healing us in our pain.

I Will Give You Rest

(Jonah 4:1-11)

"And should I not be concerned over Nineveh, the great city, in
which there are more than a hundred and twenty thousand persons
who cannot distinguish their right hand from their left, not to
mention the many cattle?"

Jonah had walked through the city of Nineveh telling all the people that
the Lord was going to destroy the city because of the sinful ways of the
people. When the people heard, they repented of their sins; the Lord had
mercy on them and spared the city. This angered Jonah. He was embar-
rassed, for he had said the city would be destroyed and then God relented.
Jonah was more interested in his reputation than in the welfare of the
people to whom he had been sent. He felt that God's justice was unfair
to him. Many times in our own lives we fail to understand the justice
of the Lord. Many times we feel we are being treated unfairly compared
with other people. We fail to understand, for example, why we might
have to suffer while others who seem less faithful sail through life. Our
Lord tells us, as he told Jonah, that we must trust him. We must trust
that his way is the right way for all people. We pray that we can accept
the trials and suffering in our lives. We pray that we may trust more fully
in the ways of the Lord, knowing that he loves each of us and desires
only good for all his children.

Were Not Our Hearts Burning!

(Hebrews 6:10-20)

"This we have as an anchor of the soul, sure and firm, which reaches
into the interior behind the veil, where Jesus has entered on our
behalf as a forerunner, becoming high priest forever according to the
order of Melchizedek."

Our lives on this earth can be very difficult. We all have crosses to bear.
Each of us struggles with temptations that can be difficult to overcome.
We all have personal suffering and sorrow in our lives. Sometimes, the
trials we face can seem overwhelming and never ending. It is in these
dark times that we must be mindful of the hope that we have in Jesus,
the hope that we have in the promises of God. In this passage we are
reminded of the constancy and the reliability of God's promise. We are
reminded of the many ways in which the Lord has already fulfilled many
of the promises he made to his people. He sent Jesus to redeem us. He
has raised Jesus up as the firstfruits of all of us who will follow. He has
been faithful to all of his promises, and we can be sure that he will continue to keep them. This must be our hope. This must be our strength.
Our trials and sufferings will continue while we are on this earth, but
we must stay strong, secure in the knowledge that God is with us, secure
in the knowledge that he will one day bring total peace and joy to our
lives when we will live in his presence forever.

I Will Give You Rest

(2 Corinthians 4:7-16)

"We are afflicted in every way, but not constrained; perplexed, but not driven to despair; persecuted, but not abandoned; struck down, but not destroyed; always carrying about in the body the dying of Jesus, so that the life of Jesus may be manifested in our mortal flesh."

Each of us has come to know that following the Lord entails hardship and is not always very easy. Just because we are followers of the Lord does not mean that we will be immune from pain and suffering. In fact, many times the opposite is true. As St. Paul tells us, as followers of Jesus we will suffer. We will have pain. We will have sorrow. But he also tells us that none of the pain and suffering will ever be able to overcome us, because we have Jesus living within us. Jesus suffered greatly in his body as he walked among us on this earth. However, we also know that through his persistent faith and trust in God, he overcame the many hardships and constraints of this world. If we are equally persistent in our faith, if we are focused on the Lord, and if we realize that every trial and suffering gives birth to our new life of joy in God, we will be raised with Jesus. As we suffer and die to ourselves, our world, and our sins, we will be raised to new life in Jesus. St. Paul reminds us that this is the mystery of God's plan for our lives. Let us give thanks and rejoice in him!

Were Not Our Hearts Burning!

(1 Kings 19:3-8)

"He prayed for death: 'This is enough, O Lord!'"

In this passage we read of the terrible anguish of the prophet Elijah as he felt that he could no longer go on doing the work of the Lord. We read of his sorrow and of his desire to give up. He asked the Lord for death. Sometimes, in our own lives we are so burdened by pain and sorrow that we feel it will be difficult to go on. We are weighed down, as was Elijah, and feel our suffering is too much to bear. We may even come to the point of almost giving up. It is in these times of extreme sorrow that we must surrender ourselves to the care and nurturing of the Lord. We must trust that he will sustain us. We read that indeed he was there to comfort Elijah. He was there to feed and nourish him. He was there to offer consolation and support. The Lord will be with us also. He will be there to comfort us. He will be there to strengthen us. He will be there to pull us through. His love, compassion, and sustenance are all that we need to overcome the burdens we carry. Even though he was suffering, Elijah opened his heart to the Lord, obeyed God's command for his life, and then experienced the healing touch of our Lord. In our sorrow we, too, must find a way to open our hearts to the Lord. We, too, must act on the Word of God as he speaks to us. When we do, we will be strengthened as was Elijah, and in God's time our sorrow will be turned into joy.

I Will Give You Rest

(Romans 8:18-38)

"We know that all things work for good for those who love God,
who are called according to his purpose."

In this imperfect world in which we live, it can be very difficult for us to understand the many trials we are forced to endure. It can be very difficult for us to understand the reasons of God for the many bad things that befall us and our world. It can be very difficult for us to understand the justice of God, which so often seems so different from our sense of justice. St. Paul exhorts us to live by faith. He explains that the only way we can come to grips with the trials and hardships in our lives is to stay close to the Lord, to love him, and to live in his love for us. He tells us that we can be strong in our faith, knowing that if we stay close to the Lord, all that happens, happens for the good of those who love God. It is hard for us to understand, but our faith must take over when our human knowledge fails. Let us pray that the Lord build up our faith in him, so that we can accept his will for our lives even when we don't understand it. Let us pray that we always stay close to the Lord, living in his love for us, so we can be assured that only goodness comes from the trials and hardships we endure in this life. Let us love the Lord in all he does, knowing that he wants only what is good for us.

Were Not Our Hearts Burning!

(Luke 1:67-79)

"And you, child, will be called prophet of the Most High, for you will go before the Lord to prepare his ways, to give his people knowledge of salvation through the forgiveness of their sins, because of the tender mercy of our God by which the daybreak from on high will visit us to shine on those who sit in darkness and death's shadow, to guard our feet into the path of peace."

This passage includes the beautiful Canticle of Zechariah. At the birth of his son John, Zechariah was filled with the Holy Spirit and uttered this beautiful confirmation of the Lord's love for his people. He prophesied that the promise of the Savior was at hand and through the Messiah we would be redeemed. Zechariah also prophesied that all who were living in darkness would be brought into the bright light of God's love. This prayer fills us with hope. Many times in our lives we find ourselves mired in darkness. We all have sorrows in our lives with which we have to deal. Keeping this prayer in our hearts will help us to endure these dark times. For we know that Jesus has come to bring salvation, he has come to bring his glorious light, and he has come to guide our feet onto the path of his peace.

I Will Give You Rest

(Mark 6:53-56)

"Whatever villages or towns or countryside he entered, they laid the sick in the marketplaces and begged him that they might touch only the tassel on his cloak; and as many as touched it were healed."

St. Mark paints a remarkable and beautiful picture of Jesus' love and compassion for his people. He tells us that wherever Jesus went, there were always crowds of people who needed comfort and healing. He tells us that just being in the presence of the Lord, just touching the tassel on his cloak, brought relief and healing to the people. Jesus continues to love all of us in just that same powerful way. He continues to have compassion for us. He longs to heal and comfort us. He longs to have us in his presence so he can minister to us, just as he ministered to the people of Israel so long ago. Jesus calls us to come into his presence. He calls us to slow down and come to him in prayer. He calls us to open our hearts to his love and healing. He wants each of us to know, personally and individually, of his love and caring for us. Let us come to the Lord in silence so that we may hear his voice. Let us be still in the presence of the Lord so that he may comfort us, minister to us, heal us, and make us aware of his great love for us.

Were Not Our Hearts Burning!

(Jeremiah 20:10-13)

"But the Lord is with me, like a mighty champion: my persecutors
will stumble, they will not triumph."

Jeremiah was under tremendous stress as he contemplated the anger
of the people against him. He knew they were plotting to kill him, and
he felt there was no place he could hide; felt powerless on his own. He
realized the only way he could control his fear and distress was to call
on the name of the Lord and then trust that the Lord would help him.
In our lives we are besieged with the stresses and fears that come with
living in our fast-paced society. We are assailed with the temptations
of the secular world in which we live. So often it feels as if we have
no control over our lives. We are sometimes reduced to living in fear
of all the trials and stress that continually plague our lives. Our Lord
calls us to learn the lesson that Jeremiah teaches us today. He calls us
to come to him. He calls us to rely on his strength and faithfulness
to help us in our struggles. God reminds us that he can conquer any
enemy. He will rescue us from the midst of our fear. Let us always rely
on the Lord. Let us surrender the helplessness we feel, the stresses
that weary us, and the temptations that plague us to the gracious and
healing love of the Lord.

I Will Give You Rest

(2 Corinthians 12:6-10)

"Three times I begged the Lord about this, that it might leave me,
but he said to me, 'My grace is sufficient for you, for power is made
perfect in weakness.'"

It is when we rely too much on our own strength and our own power that we become weak in the Lord. We may begin to become too proud to be of service to the Lord in the way in which he wants to use us. St. Paul came to know that, and he teaches us today that we, too, must come to realize it is the power of God in us that makes us strong. St. Paul tells us of an illness with which he suffered. He prayed, but the Lord never healed that affliction. Instead, the Lord used that affliction to make St. Paul stronger, to make him a more effective instrument. Many of us are afflicted with ailments or especially tough trials we must face. They may seem unbearable. We are called to realize that our Lord heals us in ways that he sees fit and that fit into his plan for us. God comes into our lives in different ways. He uses us in different ways. We are called to understand that whatever trials we must endure, the Lord is always with us. His grace is more than enough to sustain us. We are called to understand it is in our trials and weakness that we are closest to the love and compassion of the Lord. We are called to be open in our weakness, that we may be used more fully and become stronger in the grace of our God.

11

PRAY CONSTANTLY

Throughout his life on earth, Jesus taught us the importance of staying close to God in prayer. It is in prayer that we hear the Lord speaking to us as he guides our lives. It is in prayer that we open ourselves completely to our God, praising him, thanking him, and placing our needs before him. As we build our personal relationship with our Lord in prayer, he is able to help us experience his love, his healing power, and his grace in our lives. As we begin to experience God more fully, our lives can become a constant prayer to the Lord.

PRAYER

Heavenly Father, send your Spirit deep within us with the gift of a stronger prayer life. Help us to find the time to be with you in prayer, that as we experience you more fully our lives may become a constant prayer of praise to you.

Were Not Our Hearts Burning!

(Luke 18:1-8)

"Then he told them a parable about the necessity for them to pray
always without becoming weary."

During his busy life, Jesus always took time to pray to the Father. He always prayed for the faith and the strength of the apostles and for their perseverance in their mission. He continually prayed for his church and for the Father's mercy on all people. Throughout his ministry Jesus taught us the importance of prayer. Jesus reminds us that it is important for us to pray constantly and to persevere in the prayers that we make to our God. He reminds us that the Father hears all of our prayers, and he will answer our prayers in his time and in his way. Just because we do not get an immediate answer from the Lord does not mean that he has not heard or will not answer our prayer. It is important for us to continually place our needs at his feet. Then we must wait on the Lord, confident that he continues to hear us, knowing that he will answer our prayer in the way that he knows is best for us.

Pray Constantly

(Colossians 1:9-14)

"Therefore, from the day we heard this, we do not cease praying for you and asking that you may be filled with the knowledge of his will through all spiritual wisdom and understanding to live in a manner worthy of the Lord, so as to be fully pleasing, in every good work bearing fruit and growing in the knowledge of God, strengthened with every power, in accord with his glorious might, for all endurance and patience, with joy giving thanks to the Father who has made you fit to share in the inheritance of the holy ones in light."

We all need the help and grace of the Lord to be able to live as confident Christians in this secular world. Without the help of the Lord, it would be easy for us to get discouraged and then find that we have left the path on which we are being led. We may have the best intentions of following the way of Jesus, and still, without the knowledge of his grace in our lives, find that we are not doing the things that might lead us closer to the Lord. In his letter to the Colossians, St. Paul reminds us of how important it is that we pray for each other. He recounts the fact that he continually prays for those who have come to know Jesus in their lives, that they might remain strong in their faith. We, too, need the strength that prayer to the Lord brings. It is the grace received from prayer that will give us the knowledge of the bounteous grace of our God. It is the grace received from prayer that will keep us committed to the Lord and faithful to the path he has chosen for us. We receive that grace from prayer, both in praying for others and in being prayed for by others. Praying for each other is an important part of our commitment to our Lord. Let us promise to pray for each other as we all strive to know and experience the love and light of God.

Were Not Our Hearts Burning!

(Mark 1:29-39)

"Rising very early before dawn, he left and went off to a deserted place, where he prayed."

We all have very busy lives. It seems that there are just not enough hours in the day to get done all that we need to do. All of us are constantly looking for ways to trim the demands on our lives. We certainly are not looking to add more. Most times, we are sure that there is not room enough for one more demand in our busy schedules. Our Lord understands how busy we are. However, he reminds us that time for prayer is of the utmost importance for our lives. We must never be too busy for prayer, as prayer is our lifeline to our God. None of us are as busy as Jesus was as he undertook the mission to proclaim the kingdom of God. As we read Scripture, we get a good sense of the demands Jesus felt as he went about preaching, teaching, and healing. In this passage we read that Jesus woke before dawn to find time for prayer. He knew how important communion with the Father was for his life. We are called to that same understanding. He calls us to find quality time, quiet time, to be in prayer with our God. Like Jesus, we must make a commitment to prayer. Jesus knew and teaches us that it is in prayer that we learn of God's plan for us. It is in prayer that we are empowered to live and proclaim the kingdom of God on earth. Prayer is our special time with our Creator. Certainly, that is time well spent!

Pray Constantly

(Mark 2:18-22)

"But the days will come when the bridegroom is taken away from them, and then they will fast on that day."

We are all called to prayer and repentance. One of the ways by which we can atone for our sins and pray to the Lord for his grace and guidance is through fasting. Jesus himself fasted as an offering to God after his baptism. He was ready to begin his public ministry and was looking for confirmation and guidance from the Father. As he withdrew from the world and all of its bounty, he could more easily see the will of God for his life. He could more readily discern the path his ministry was to take. It is good for us to get away from the world and its bounty. Unlike Jesus who had no sin, it is a way for us to stay mindful of our sinfulness and to atone for those sins we have committed. Fasting is a way for us to offer a sacrifice to God. It is a way for us to open our hearts to his plan for our lives. It is a way for us to feed and nourish our souls instead of our bodies. It is a reminder to us of the importance of caring for and nourishing our souls. The Lord calls us to consider this beautiful form of sacrifice and prayer. We know that as we consider and add some kind of fasting to our prayer lives, the Lord will bless our efforts. He will fill us with his grace and love.

Were Not Our Hearts Burning!

(Matthew 9:32-38)

"Then he said to his disciples, 'The harvest is abundant but the laborers are few; so ask the master of the harvest to send out laborers for his harvest.'"

Jesus reminds us that there has been, and always will be, a need for shepherds to help lead his flock. He tells us that as the sheep of his flock one of our duties is to pray that God will send more laborers for the harvest. We know that at this time in history there is a great need for more shepherds. There are so many who need to hear the Word of God. There are so many who need the guidance and leadership of the Lord's chosen shepherds. In this age, our lifestyles do little to promote vocations to God's service. We know we need more people committed to God's service, but become hesitant when talking about ourselves or our own children. Because the values are so different, it is sometimes thought that a religious vocation will somehow keep a person from reaching his or her full potential. Our Lord tells us that there is nothing further from the truth. There is no higher calling than to work in the service of the Lord. Let us pray that our attitudes regarding religious vocations change, and that our God will continue to send and bless special people who will lead, teach, and help pasture his sheep.

Pray Constantly

(Luke 17:11-19)

"Jesus said in reply, 'Ten were cleansed, were they not? Where are the other nine?'"

This passage recounts the cleansing of ten lepers. All ten were healed and sent on their way, but only one came back to thank Jesus for healing him. Not only that, but the one who returned was not of the house of Israel. Those who should have known better did not return to thank Jesus. Jesus teaches that we must never take for granted the love and goodness of our God. As we pray to the Lord, we are never afraid to ask for many things. Jesus exhorts us to also be faithful in prayers of thanksgiving to God for prayers answered and blessings received. As Christians we are very aware of all the Lord has given us. We are very aware of his mercy and his desire to answer our prayers. We see and experience the goodness of our God every day. We are called to come to the Lord with grateful hearts. We are called to be a rejoicing and thankful people, as the Lord continues to act powerfully in our lives. We have so much to be thankful for. Let us never forget it. Let us always come to the Lord in thanksgiving for his love and goodness in our lives.

Were Not Our Hearts Burning!

(1 Kings 8:22-30)

"If the heavens and the highest heavens cannot contain you, how much less this temple which I have built."

King Solomon eloquently expresses the thoughts that we all have in our hearts. He proclaims the majesty and the glory of God. He marvels at the love the Lord continually shows his people, and how the Lord, who cannot be contained, is so powerfully present in their lives. He is truly humbled by the love and greatness of the Lord. The prayer of King Solomon should be one that we keep close to our hearts, for we, too, can be no less humbled by the love and majesty of our God. We continue to experience the powerful presence of our Lord in our lives and in our world. We experience his love in our lives every day. We can only marvel at all the Lord does for us who are so unworthy. He even sent his Son, while we were still sinners, to redeem us and to reconcile us to our Father. Prayers of praise should always be included when we speak to our Lord in prayer. Prayers of praise and worship enhance our humility before the Lord, and it is in that humility that we become aware of the greatness of our God and our dependence on him for our existence. He is our God. We are the people he calls his own. Praise be to God!

Pray Constantly

(Philippians 4:4-7)

"Have no anxiety at all, but in everything, by prayer and petition, with thanksgiving, make your requests known to God."

St. Paul exhorts us to rejoice always and in everything. He tells us that we should have no anxiety. This may seem impossible for us. It may be easy for us to just read this passage and pass it off as sounding nice, but much too difficult to put into practice. We live in a world that is filled with anxiety. Anxiety is a major part of our lives in this society. There seems to be so much to worry about, so much about which to be fearful, so much that stands in the way of true peace in our lives. Yet, here is St. Paul telling us not to be anxious about anything. How can we put into practice what St. Paul advocates in this passage? He tells us there is only one answer. He tells us that we can relieve all of our anxiety through constant prayer. He tells us that we should offer in prayer everything that we are, to surrender everything in our lives to the care of the Lord. Finally, he tells us that we must always live our lives in thanksgiving to the Lord. We must thank him constantly for life and for his powerful presence in it, in the good times and the bad, knowing that he will take care of us for he is our loving Father. Lord, we thank you always!

Were Not Our Hearts Burning!

(Matthew 6:5-15)

"Your Father knows what you need before you ask him."

Our God created us and knows all of our needs. He knows the desire of our hearts even before we are aware of it. Yet, we are still called to pray. We are called to praise and glorify the Lord in prayer. We are called to place all of our needs at the feet of our most gracious God. We are called to prayers of thanksgiving to the Lord, who gives us all good things. We are called to persevere in all forms of prayer, so that our lives become a constant prayer to the Lord. We know that the Lord has no real need of our praise or our prayers, yet he delights in all that we offer him. The prayers that we do offer are for our own benefit. Our prayers keep us ever mindful of our dependence on God. They keep us ever mindful of the goodness and the majesty of our God. And as we pray for others, prayer keeps us ever mindful of our call to share and help each other on our journey on earth. Jesus prayed constantly to the Father during his life on this earth, and in this passage he teaches the apostles how to pray. Let us pray for a new gift of prayer in our lives, that we may gain wisdom and grace through our prayers, and that our lives more closely follow Jesus' life, lived in such closeness with the Father.

Pray Constantly

(John 21:1-14)

"So the disciple whom Jesus loved said to Peter, 'It is the Lord.'"

In this resurrection story, the disciples did not at first recognize Jesus. It was only when the Lord did something that was familiar to them that they recognized him. If they had not been so familiar with him, they might have failed to recognize him. Jesus calls us to get to know him in our lives. He calls us to communicate with him in prayer so that we may become familiar with his ways. He wants us to become familiar with the way he speaks to us and acts in our lives. If we do not have a good and active prayer life, if we do not strive to see Jesus in our lives, we will stand a good chance of failing to recognize him when he acts in our lives. It is only when we become familiar with how Jesus speaks to us and acts in our lives that we become confident in the way and the will of God for us. It is in becoming more familiar with Jesus that our faith is built up and we become more confident on our journey to the life of holiness to which we are called. Let us pray for a stronger personal relationship with the Lord in our prayer lives. Let us come to know, hear, and see him more clearly.

Were Not Our Hearts Burning!

(Acts 1:15-26)

"Then they prayed, 'You, Lord, who know the hearts of all, show which one of these two you have chosen to take the place in this apostolic ministry from which Judas turned away to go to his own place.'"

In this passage we read of the apostles' decision to replace Judas. As Jesus lived his life, the apostles had observed that he prayed often. He prayed in praise of the Father, in thanksgiving to the Father, and for guidance and help as he furthered the plan of God on earth. This lesson of prayer was not lost on the apostles, and it must not be lost on us. Before the apostles made this big decision, they prayed for God's guidance and help. As Christians and followers of the example of the apostles, we are called to bring God into all of the decisions that affect our lives. We are called to pray for God's help and intercession in the decisions that affect our own lives, our families, our communities, and our world. The apostles taught us that the Lord is interested in all areas of our lives. The more we let the Lord into our lives, the more he can help us succeed. Our Lord calls us to pray often and in all situations, coming to him as individuals, families, and communities. Let us answer God's call and follow the example of the apostles to be people of prayer, always opening our lives to our Almighty God.

Pray Constantly

(Mark 9:2-10)

"Then Peter said to Jesus in reply, 'Rabbi, it is good that we
are here!'"

As Jesus was transfigured in the presence of the apostles, we can only
imagine what they thought as they saw the Lord in all of his glory. We
know that they were completely awestruck and amazed. St. Peter was in
such a state of joy that he wanted to remain with Jesus on that mountain.
But Jesus told him no, that they must return to complete the mission for
which he had been sent. Many of us experience the peace and joy that
St. Peter felt when we are in prayer with the Lord, alive in his presence.
We want to remain in that state with Jesus always. But Jesus reminds
us that most of us are called to live our lives in this world, a world that
can definitely be a distraction and a stumbling block to a close relationship with the Lord. Jesus calls us to use our times of prayer to fill our
lives with his strength and grace so we will be prepared for the desert
times the world offers. He tells us we must take the experiences of his
love and grace into a world that so badly needs his touch and healing
power and to share that which we receive from him. We are called to
bring that peace to bear in our world so all might come to know the
glory of our Lord.

12

Persevere
In My Love

We have our life in the Lord. He is our hope and our joy. As our society goes further and further down the road of secularism, we are called to remain strong in the Lord. As temptations multiply and grow stronger to follow the way of the world, we are called to remain always in the love and light of our God.

Prayer

Most powerful Lord, give us the grace and strength to persevere in following your way for our lives. Help us in times of temptation. Give us the wisdom to understand that it is only in you that we will find true happiness and peace.

Were Not Our Hearts Burning!

(Deuteronomy 10:12-22)

"For the Lord, your God, is the God of gods, the Lord of lords, the great God, mighty and awesome, who has no favorites, accepts no bribes; who executes justice for the orphan and the widow, and befriends the alien, feeding and clothing him."

Our God calls us to change our hearts, to amend our lives, and conform to the way of the Lord. For there is no other way that we may attain the goal of heaven. In our society much emphasis is placed on getting ahead at any cost. In many cases the ends justify the means. We often bargain and cajole to get the things we want. The Lord tells us that we must be different in dealing with him. He will accept only sincere repentance and sincere efforts to follow his commandments and his way for our lives. He plays no favorites. He will not bargain with us. He knows our hearts better than we do. He understands our weaknesses and strengths. We may be able to fool ourselves, but we can never fool God. Therefore, let us resolve to make a sincere effort to mend our ways. Let us pray for the strength and courage to be honest with ourselves in dealing with the Lord and following his way for us. Let us heed God's call to love and serve him in this life, to make him our number one priority and so receive his peace in our lives.

Persevere In My Love

(Ephesians 5:15-20)

"Watch carefully then how you live, not as foolish persons but as wise, making the most of the opportunity, because the days are evil."

St. Paul reminds us that we must be ever vigilant, watching how we live our lives in a world that is opposed to the way we are called to live. Trials and temptations abound, and if we are not always careful we can easily fall into a way of life that is opposed to the Lord's way for us. St. Paul tells us that we must be wise in the way in which we live our lives. He tells us that we become wise by understanding the way the Lord desires us to live our lives. We become wise by understanding the trials and temptations of this life, how insidious the temptations are that befall us, and recognizing the ways the world tries to seduce us. It is in that knowledge and wisdom that we have the strength to prevail. This wisdom and knowledge come from the Lord. The Lord will always help us in our struggle and will grant us his wisdom and knowledge as we stay close to him in prayer and strive to lead holy lives. Let us do our part. Let us continue to strive to live in the wisdom and knowledge of God through the power of the Holy Spirit. Let us watch carefully and live as wise persons, knowing that the Lord will be with us always.

Were Not Our Hearts Burning!

(John 6:60-69)

"Then many of his disciples who were listening said, 'This saying is hard; who can accept it?'"

In the secular world in which we live, many of the commandments and teachings of Jesus seem very difficult. They certainly fly in the face of the lifestyles that are prevalent in our society. If we aspire to those lifestyles, which are so popular, it can be very difficult to accept and live the teachings of Jesus. As we read that some of the disciples of Jesus had a very difficult time with some of his teachings, we come to know that this dilemma of faith and lifestyles has been with us throughout salvation history. Some of the disciples of Jesus found his teachings just too hard to follow. What is important for us to realize is that Jesus did not change his teachings in order to satisfy those disciples. He sadly let them go. In our lives, when we come into conflict with the laws of God, too often we want to change those laws rather than change our lives. We want to update the laws of God so that they fit better the lifestyles to which we aspire. Jesus tells us that it can never be that way. His Word and his law are forever. If we find our lifestyles in conflict with the laws of God, we must change. We must conform our lives to the laws and teachings of the Lord, not the other way around. Jesus tells us that if we do, we will find peace and happiness in him.

Persevere In My Love

(Haggai 2:1-9)

"For thus says the Lord of hosts: one moment yet, a little while, and
I will shake the heavens and the earth, the sea and the dry land. I
will shake the nations, and the treasures of all the nations will come
in, and I will fill this house with glory, says the Lord of hosts."

In this imperfect world, with all of its trials, sorrows, and the many trag-
edies that are so hard to understand, it is easy to become discouraged.
Sometimes it seems as if the world is spinning out of control and our
lives spinning with it. As we strive to live out the will of God for our
lives, it can sometimes seem as though we are fighting a losing battle.
We can certainly identify with the Jewish people in this passage from
the Old Testament book of the prophet Haggai. It has been such a long
time since they have seen the glory of the temple of the Lord. They feel
lost. They feel as if God has abandoned them. We, too, sometimes have
those feelings of frustration. But the Lord tells us that those feelings
of frustration and of being lost will last only for a moment in time. He
calls on us to rely on our faith and to trust in him, for he will shake the
heavens and the earth, and it is he and all who persevere in his way who
will triumph. Ours is a God of power and majesty. His plan for us and for
our world will prevail, and we who live his will for our lives and follow
his way will triumph with him. And so, we take heart. We live in hope,
knowing that our God will be triumphant, and that he will lift us up, and
we will reign forever with our Lord, Jesus, in his heavenly kingdom.

Were Not Our Hearts Burning!

(Luke 16:9-15)

"The person who is trustworthy in very small matters is also trustworthy in great ones; and the person who is dishonest in very small matters is also dishonest in great ones."

In our society, the lines between good and evil have become more and more blurred. Instead of being black and white, most things seem to be shades of gray. This can make it difficult to live a good solid Christian life. We can begin to lose the idea that there truly is a difference between right and wrong. Jesus reminds us that he has taught us the way to live in order for us to remain close to the Father. He reminds us that we must pay attention to detail. Every letter of the law that he has taught us is important if we are to live in the peace of God's light. The way of the world is to minimize the details, to blur the lines between right and wrong. The way of the world in so many instances tells us that the ends justify the means. Jesus tells us that not paying attention to every detail of living a good life cannot be our way. He has given us the example of his own life, that we may pattern our lives after him and stay the course on all that we have been taught. Let us pray that we are always trustworthy in every detail of living our Christian lives. Let us be a beacon of light to those in our world so that the love and goodness of our God can overcome the indifference of our broken world.

Persevere In My Love

(Acts 18:1-8)

"Crispus, the synagogue official, came to believe in the Lord along
with his entire household, and many of the Corinthians who heard
believed and were baptized."

St. Paul was very persistent. Many times as he preached the Word of God
to the people he was rebuffed. Yet, he never stopped preaching, never
stopped sharing with others what he experienced in Jesus. He never
stopped striving to follow the path that the Lord had laid out for him.
As he persevered, his efforts were rewarded and many came to believe.
We must also persevere in our faith and in our calling. We must never
give up following the path the Lord has laid out for us. We must live
out our faith no matter the obstacle, no matter how many roadblocks
are put before us, no matter the temptations of worldly lifestyles, and no
matter how often we fail to see immediate results or rewards. We must
never give up praising the Lord in word and action. We must never give
up on sharing with others all that we have experienced in Jesus. Just as
St. Paul was rewarded, our efforts will be rewarded by the Lord as we
experience his peace and joy in our lives.

Were Not Our Hearts Burning!

(Genesis 19:1-29)

"As soon as they had been brought outside, he was told, 'Flee for your life! Don't look back or stop anywhere on the Plain.'"

This passage is the familiar story of Lot and his family fleeing the punishment of God on Sodom and Gomorrah. Lot and his family were led out of the city and told to flee for their lives. They were told not to look back, but to keep their eyes focused on the journey ahead. We know that Lot's wife did look back and was turned into a pillar of salt and never reached her goal of freedom. Our Lord calls us to follow him closely and stay focused on the road ahead. He calls us to live in his light through his grace and his Word. He calls us to keep going forward on our journey with him and not succumb to the fears that are behind us. In his mercy he has led us out of the darkness of sin. He has led us out of the darkness of our human weakness and into the strength of his love. It is when we look back on our many failures, instead of relying on God's love and mercy in our lives, that we fall back into that darkness and fear. The light and grace of God are always before us. Let us pray for the grace to keep our eyes focused on the light of God's grace, which leads us. Let us pray for the grace to accept God's love and mercy in our lives so that we have no reason to look back, but have every reason to march forward with Jesus as our Standard Bearer.

Persevere In My Love

(1 John 2:28–3:3)

"Everyone who has this hope based on him makes himself pure, as he is pure."

It is easier for us to persevere in our faith when we are reminded of just who we are in Jesus and how we fit into the family of God. St. John reminds us of the love and goodness of the Lord, and reminds us that as we reflect on God's love we will be able to do nothing less than stay true to our Christian calling. He reminds us that through Jesus, we have truly become the sons and daughters of God. He explains that, although we are not sure what we shall become after this life on earth, our God has a special place prepared for us and we will live in the joy and peace of his presence. Finally, St. John exhorts us to keep all of these things constantly in our minds so that we are more easily able to persevere in the life we have chosen in Christ. Let us thank the Lord every day for the gift of his only begotten Son, Jesus. Let us thank him for the wisdom and knowledge he bestows upon us, so that we are able to comprehend his great love for us. Let us pray that in the wisdom and knowledge he has given us, we are able to stay strong in our commitment to follow him and always stay focused on the path he has chosen for us.

Were Not Our Hearts Burning!

(Numbers 21:4-9)

"But with their patience worn out by the journey, the people complained against God and Moses, 'Why have you brought us up from Egypt to die in this desert, where there is no food or water?'"

As we read of the journey of the Israelites, as they were led out of Egypt and into the desert on the way to the promised land, we cannot help but notice that they complained loudly and often. Whenever some small hardship would arise, the people complained against God and Moses, sometimes wishing they had never left their former lives as slaves in Egypt. The Lord continued to care for them and provided all that they needed, but it seems they were seldom happy with what they had and quickly forgot all the wonders the Lord was working for them. We are called to examine our own lives in the light of the Israelites' journey with the Lord. The Lord has led us out of the darkness of our sin and continues to care for us and provide all that we need in this life. Although we live in his glorious light, it is sometimes a struggle to remain there. Like the Israelites, we will suffer hardship. The Lord calls us to trust in his care for us. Instead of complaining about all our difficulties as we strive to lead good Christian lives, we must remember that the Lord is constantly providing for us. We are called to lift to him our prayers of praise and joy, knowing that he is always there for us as we continue our earthly journey, constant in our efforts to follow our God more closely.

Persevere In My Love

(Acts 5:27-33)

"But Peter and the apostles said in reply, 'We must obey God rather than men.'"

Standing before the elders and leaders of the Jewish people, the apostles were certainly in danger of being jailed, or even worse, put to death as Jesus had been. Yet, they did not waver. Through the strength and courage they had in the Holy Spirit, they were able to withstand the fear of the situation and follow the call of the Lord. The apostles continued to obey God in the face of all obstacles. We face the decision of whether we will follow God or follow some other way every day of our lives. Our lives are filled with choices of not only whom we will follow, but which path we will take. We are called to constant reflection in our lives, to make sure that we are obeying our God and following him wherever he leads us. Thankfully, we do not usually have to worry about being put in jail or dying for following the Lord, but our choices are just as important. Because of the freedoms we enjoy, we run the risk of being led away from the Lord in more subtle ways. Let us make sure that we always make the choice to obey the Lord. Let us remain strong in our faith, never choosing anyone or anything that might lead us away from our God.

Were Not Our Hearts Burning!

(John 15:18-21)

"If the world hates you, realize that it hated me first."

Jesus died for the sins of all men and women. He arose from the dead to destroy death and win the victory for all men and women. Jesus knew, however, that there would be some who would turn their backs on the salvation that he had won. There were some who would continue to live in darkness, never opening their hearts to the light of the Lord. Jesus reminds the apostles, and us, that there would still be hate in the world for him and his teachings. There would still be persecution for those who followed him. Jesus himself had suffered at the hands of those who refused to embrace the life of love that Jesus offers to all. He tells us that it would be no different for the apostles, who were carrying on his mission after his ascension, or for us who continue to carry on his mission today. He reminds us that all we can do is live our own lives in his light and love and share with others the goodness and love that we have experienced in Jesus. He tells us that all we can do is offer each person the invitation to "Come and see" so that all people have the opportunity to embrace the light, an opportunity to have new life in Jesus, our Savior.

Persevere In My Love

(John 16:20-23)

"Amen, amen, I say to you, you will weep and mourn, while the world rejoices; you will grieve, but your grief will become joy."

Jesus reminds us that our way, as we strive to follow him, is a very different way than the way of the world. He explains that his way may seem more difficult as we strive to forsake the temptations of this world. However, if we persevere in the way of truth, the difficulty will turn into joy, consternation will transform into peace. Each of us is very aware of the lure that our secular world has on us. We have all had experience with those who think that the way of the Lord is not conducive to the times or that God's laws are out of step with technology. The arguments seem persuasive, and when the majority holds views that contradict our own beliefs, it can become very painful to stay the course. Pain and grief can sometimes be the price that we must pay to stay true to the way of God, which is always the same and will never change. Our Lord encourages us to remain strong, to stay the course. He promises that when we do, we will triumph over the way of the world. He promises that peace and joy will be our reward.

Were Not Our Hearts Burning!

(1 John 2:18-21)

"Children, it is the last hour, and just as you heard that the antichrist was coming, so now many antichrists have appeared."

It is so important that we stay firm in our faith. As St. John reminds us, we have been given the gift of faith. We have been given the gifts of knowledge and wisdom that point the way to Christ. We must never squander these gifts. There are many different ways and philosophies in this world, many fads that catch the fancy of the people. Leaders abound who preach all kinds of strange teachings. Some are out there and are easily dismissed, but others are more subtle and insidious. They may have a ring of truth to them. Some may seem easier to follow than the way we have chosen to follow. Some may seem more compatible to the way we live in our society. But, St. John reminds us that there is only one true way. We must continue to follow that way. We must never get caught up in other teachings, no matter how easy or popular. We remain strong in our faith by living it every day. We remain strong in our faith by immersing ourselves in the Word of God in Scripture. We remain strong in our faith through prayer. We remain strong in our faith through association with other believers in our communities. The Lord has shown us the way. May we never become lost.

Persevere In My Love

(Malachi 3:1-4)

"For he is like the refiner's fire, or like the fuller's lye."

God sent his Son into the world to show us the way. He died for our sins and forever broke the bonds of sin and death. He is the face of God, our Father. We know that the life of Jesus was not an easy one. He stood against many of the laws and customs of the day. He associated with people who were outcasts. His life was one of contrast to the way in which most people of the day were living. That is the same life to which we are called in Christ. He calls us to stand against all that we know is wrong, all that comes against the plan of God for his people. He calls us to befriend and assist those who are outcasts. He calls us to live lives which stand in contrast to the lives lived by most of the people of this age. That is not an easy thing for us to do. It requires strength and sacrifice. It requires dying to ourselves, which is painful and difficult. It requires standing apart from the crowd and at times being an object of derision. Yet, this is exactly the way of life to which we are called. Through the prophet Malachi our Lord tells us that we will be tested. We will be changed as we open our lives to the power of the Lord. We are promised, however, that if we succeed in following the Lord, if we allow him to test and change us, we will come out stronger, happier, and more at peace. We will be one with our Creator God.

13

WHERE TWO OR MORE ARE GATHERED

Our Lord tells us that where two or more are gathered, he will be powerfully present. The aspect of community was so important in the foundation and building of Christ's church. The importance of community is just as strong for us today. There is strength in community. There is power in community. There is faith sharing and building in community. There is hope in community. The Lord is present in community.

PRAYER

Ever-present Lord, be with us in our communities as we gather together to praise you, to implore your help, to laugh, cry, and share with each other. Be with us in our communities as we build in each other the faith, hope, and love we so need in these difficult times.

Were Not Our Hearts Burning!

(Acts 4:32-37)

"The community of believers was of one heart and mind, and no one claimed that any of his possessions was his own, but they had everything in common."

Because of the persecution of the early Christians and because the Way was still very new to many people, the obvious solution was that the faithful should live and learn as a community. This they did, taking care of each other, strengthening each other, and helping to sustain each other's faith as God showered his gifts upon them through the power of the Holy Spirit. Our society is so different. Independence is king. Far from being of one heart and mind, our society fosters diversity. This diversity is apparent in all facets of our lives. Diversity can certainly be a good thing, since we are all different and unique individuals, pursuing many different goals and having different passions. On the other hand, this spirit of independence works against the power of community in the area of our faith. Community is so important, as through community we are encouraged to live strong Christian lives, forsaking more easily the temptations of the world. Community strengthens and nourishes our faith, a faith that continues to be battered by our society's move towards secularism. Let us rejoice in community and strive to keep community an important part of our lives and our faith, trusting that God will provide all we need to nurture and strengthen each other as we continue to walk with the Lord.

Where Two Or More Are Gathered

(Philippians 3:17–4:11)

"Join with others in being imitators of me, brothers, and observe those who thus conduct themselves according to the model you have in us."

In our world, little value is placed on the virtues that are so important to living a strong life in Christ. There are many examples of how to succeed in the world, how to make money, and how to take advantage of all of the pleasures this world offers. St. Paul reminds us of the importance of good role models in our spiritual lives. He tells us that with much stacked against us as we strive to live lives of holiness, we must find good examples whose lives will help guide us. St. Paul calls on us to imitate him and others who have followed the way of the Lord in their lives. We are called to reflect upon those whom we know are committed to living a life in Christ and pattern our lives after them. That is why community is so important for us. We are called to surround ourselves with others who share our same goals. As some members of our communities become examples for us, we can become examples for others, all modeling our lives after the example of Jesus. Let us thank the Lord for his saints, living and dead, who continue to provide motivation for us. Let us thank the Lord that the example of their lives provides patterns for our own lives.

Were Not Our Hearts Burning!

(Acts 13:13-25)

"After the reading of the law and the prophets, the synagogue officials sent word to them, 'My brothers, if one of you has a word of exhortation for the people, please speak.'"

On his travels proclaiming the Word of God to the people, St. Paul was welcomed by few of the leaders of the Jewish community. St. Paul had been raised a Jew, and because he had community ties with the Jews of the region, he attempted to take part as often as possible in the community. Community was always important to St. Paul, and in this passage we are presented with the importance of community in the lives of the people of God. The synagogue officials asked St. Paul to lift up the entire community with words of encouragement. The leaders recognized that it is important to be lifted up and affirmed by the actions and prayers of others. We still have that need today. Community can be so important to our spiritual growth. We all need the support and inspiration to live the best Christian lives of which we are capable. Through community we receive the help and inspiration we need to remain strong in our faith. Our Lord calls us to be a strong part of our Christian communities, both inspiring others and being inspired to live always the faith we profess.

Where Two Or More Are Gathered

(Romans 6:3-9)

"For if we have grown into union with him through a death like his,
we shall also be united with him in the resurrection."

All of us who have been baptized in the Lord are one family. We are all part of the chosen family of God. We are all members of the mystical body of Christ. We are united in life and in death. Those saints who have gone before us have left this world, but are still part of the one body. We are called to continue to pray for them that they may be raised up on the last day, and that the body of Christ remains strong. St. Paul explains that there is a union of all who have died with Christ in baptism. He reminds us that as we share in his death, we will also share in his resurrection. When Christ comes again, his mystical body will be a whole and complete sacrifice with Christ as the head to the praise and glory of God the Father. Let us remember that we, as well as all who have gone before us, are one in Christ. Let us continue to pray for the faithful departed, that the Lord have mercy on all of the members of his one body, and that in his most gracious mercy, we all attain the promise of Christ to share in his resurrection on the last day.

14

MAKE DISCIPLES OF ALL NATIONS

Our gracious Lord continues to give us so much. He is our Savior. He continues to love us, to heal us, and to shower us with his grace and mercy. He continues to build us up and bring peace and joy to our lives. Jesus has given us the command to share all that he gives us. Until he comes again, we are his hands, his eyes, his feet. He wants to use us to open the hearts of others, so that he can touch them and bring to the lives of all people the wondrous gifts that he continually gives us.

PRAYER

Most precious Jesus, you have commanded that we share the Good News of salvation with all the world. You have commanded that we share with others the many wonderful and life-changing gifts we have received from you. Through the power of your Holy Spirit, give us a new boldness in you. Help us to better realize the power in our own stories of your love, so that we can share them with all in our lives that everyone can experience your love and the power of your grace.

Were Not Our Hearts Burning!

(Isaiah 60:1-6, Ephesians 3:1-6)

"Nations shall walk by your light, and kings by your
shining radiance."

The Lord is king over all peoples. Our God sent his only Son to this world, and in him all people have been redeemed. All people have been reconciled with the Father through Jesus Christ. All people have been made sons and daughters of God in Jesus' name. The promise of God given to Abraham and his descendants is our promise and the promise of all people. As St. Paul tells us, that which was hidden has been made known to all in Jesus' name through the power of the Holy Spirit. As Christians, we have become the light for others who do not yet know Jesus. We have become the star by which people are led to the joy that is Jesus Christ. Just as we have been led and helped to grow in our faith by the example and faith of others, it is now our turn to lead still others to Christ by the power of our faith. We live in the light of the Lord because of the faithfulness of others who came before us. It is now our turn to be faithful to the one true Light who is Jesus. Jesus desires that it now be our faithfulness that brings others into the beauty of his light. Let us ask the Lord for his grace and strength that we might lead others to him by our faith. Let us thank our loving God for bringing us into his marvelous light and giving us the most precious gift of salvation in Jesus' name.

Make Disciples Of All Nations

(2 Corinthians 9:6-11)

"Consider this: whoever sows sparingly will also reap sparingly, and whoever sows bountifully will also reap bountifully."

Our God loves to pour out his grace and blessings upon all of his children. He loves each of us unconditionally, and provides generously for our well-being. St. Paul explains that God will never be outdone in kindness, goodness, and generosity. He exhorts us to first look at God's generosity toward us, and then to imitate the love and care which we are shown. He reminds us that God is not stingy with us in any way, so we must not be stingy in sharing the love and blessings we receive with others in our lives. In fact, St. Paul tells us that the more we share with others the gifts of God that we have received, the more we will receive in return. We are called to trust fully in the Lord to provide for our needs. If we lack that trust, we will be afraid to share with others that which we have received. However, when we trust in the Lord's goodness, we will always be open to sharing all that we receive, for we know the Lord will provide for all our needs. Our God is so good. He invites us to live boldly in his love for us. He calls us to be a joyful and rejoicing people, always inviting others to share in his bounty.

Were Not Our Hearts Burning!

(John 1:19-28)

"He said: 'I am the voice of one crying out in the desert, make straight the way of the Lord,' as Isaiah the prophet said."

St. John the Baptist was the herald of Christ for the Jewish people. They had been waiting so long for the peace and joy that the Messiah was to bring. He was a voice proclaiming joy in a desert of sorrow and hopelessness. He was the conscience of a people calling for repentance and reconciliation with God. He pointed the way to the Lord. There is still much sorrow and hopelessness in our world. There is still a need for voices proclaiming peace and joy. There are still so many who need to hear of the love and mercy of God. There are many who need to hear the call to repentance and reconciliation with God. There are many waiting for someone to point the way to the Lord. We as the church are that voice. We are called to proclaim the salvation of the Lord by living the love of God in our lives. We are called to point the way to the Lord and proclaim to others his love and mercy, by sharing with others all that God has done for us. Our God is power and majesty, love and mercy, peace and joy. He is hope in a world that is filled with hopelessness. Let us proclaim his salvation. Let us proclaim the Good News to a world that is starved for good news.

Make Disciples Of All Nations

(Acts 22:1-21)

"Then he said, 'The God of our ancestors designated you to know
his will, to see the Righteous One, and to hear the sound of his
voice; for you will be his witness before all to what you have seen
and heard.'"

St. Paul was called to be a witness for Christ. Jesus called him out of
the darkness of his former way of life, and by his grace led him into a
new life. St. Paul opened his heart to the Lord, and in that moment he
felt the power of the love of God. It was a power of love that he could
never forget. It was a power of love that changed his life forever. It was
a power of love that he could not help but share with all people whom
he met. We are called to open our hearts to the life-changing power of
God's love. No matter what our circumstances, no matter where we are
on our journey of faith, the Lord can change our lives. He will continue
to draw us closer to himself. We, too, are called to be witnesses for Christ.
We are called to share the love that we have experienced with all in our
lives. St. Paul had a compelling and powerful story to share. His was
a unique life. Each of us has a story of our own to tell. Each of us has
experienced and continues to experience Jesus in unique and wonderful
ways. We have opened our hearts and continue to open our hearts and
lives to Jesus in unique and different ways. Our lives, lived for Christ,
can be a special witness to others. Let us pray for the grace and courage
to accept the call of Jesus to be his witnesses. Let us always be ready to
share his love with all that our Lord may reign in every heart.

Were Not Our Hearts Burning!

(Mark 7:24-30)

"He entered a house and wanted no one to know about it, but he could not escape notice."

Because of his holiness and the many miracles and wonders which Jesus continued to perform, it was difficult for him to go anywhere without being noticed. His compassion and the power of his message led people to follow him, to try and always be near him. Great crowds gathered wherever he went. People wanted to hear and come to know the love of God. They wanted to know that God cared about them. We in this age are the very same. We are drawn to the Lord, and to the men and women who model God's love in their lives. There are many who long to know the Lord in their lives, to know that he cares about them. As we come to know the Lord and move closer to him, people will be able to see that in us. They will be drawn to us, wanting to be reassured in their faith and hope. The light of Jesus will shine out through us. It will not be able to be hidden. Jesus calls us to let the light of his love shine in us. He calls us to model for others the love we have come to know in him. He calls us to help build up the faith and hope of all with whom we come into contact. Jesus is the Light of the world! Let the light of Jesus shine in us!

Make Disciples Of All Nations

(Micah 5:1-4)

"He shall stand firm and shepherd his flock by the strength of the Lord, in the majestic name of the Lord, his God; and they shall remain, for now his greatness shall reach to the ends of the earth; he shall be peace."

We have truly seen the greatness of our God. The prophet Micah recounts for us that the greatness of the Lord our God will be known throughout all the earth. His love and power will be known through his only begotten Son, Jesus. This prophecy has been made manifest. We have seen that the name of Jesus resounds throughout the whole world. Even though we have seen this prophecy come true in Jesus, we know that it is still continuing to be fulfilled throughout the world as there are many who still do not know the Lord. There are also many who have known the Lord and have fallen away from him. Jesus calls us to be a part of the fulfillment of this prophecy as we make manifest the greatness of the Lord by our words and actions. Let us pray that this prophecy continues to be fulfilled in all of its glory. Let us continue to show by the example of our lives that our God is great and majestic, that he shepherds his flock with love and care, and that he has saved us by sending his Son, Jesus Christ, into the world.

Were Not Our Hearts Burning!

(Zechariah 8:20-23)

"Thus says the Lord of hosts: there shall yet come peoples, the inhabitants of many cities; and the inhabitants of one city shall approach those of another, and say, come! Let us go to implore the favor of the Lord; and, 'I too will go to seek the Lord.'"

Jesus taught and preached in a very small area of the world. He saw relatively few people throughout his life on earth. He commanded that those who were closest to him go to the ends of the earth, bringing the gospel to all people. Through the power of the Holy Spirit, the apostles' faith grew, and they were able to reach many more people with the good news of salvation. In this passage the prophet Zechariah receives a word from the Lord that reflects what is going on in our world today. That tiny seed of faith, planted in such a faraway place in a time so long ago, is flourishing today. The Word of God is being spread throughout the world to billions of people. We are a part of that action of God. We are a part of God's action as we live our lives in the light and truth of the Lord. We are a part of God's action as we share with others in our lives what the Lord has done for us. We are a part of God's action when we support the missionary efforts of so many around the world. We are part of something glorious and majestic. We are part of the whole family of God. Praise you, Lord!

Make Disciples Of All Nations

(Matthew 25:31-46)

"For I was hungry and you gave me food, I was thirsty and you gave
me drink, a stranger and you welcomed me, naked and you clothed
me, ill and you cared for me, in prison and you visited me."

Ours is a faith of love and action. Our Lord healed and consoled people.
He loved people and took care of their needs. He respected all people
and had a special place in his heart for the poor and those who were
marginalized by society. Jesus calls us to continue his work. He calls us
to experience his love and the life-giving power of our faith, and then
share that with others. He calls us to experience the positive power of
God's goodness and use that power to change the suffering and nega-
tivism in our world. Our faith must be a positive force for good in the
world. Many see Christianity as confining and limiting. Some feel that
it is exclusionary. Nothing is further from the truth. Our God loves
and cares for all people, and as his followers we are called to love and
care for all people as he does. We can show the strength of our faith by
hearing God's call to action and love. We can model the love of God for
the whole world by the way we live our lives, respecting the dignity of
every person by loving and caring for all. Let us pray for the grace to
live our faith in the strong and life-giving power that God desires for
all his followers. Let us pray for the grace to share God's love and peace
with all of his children.

Were Not Our Hearts Burning!

(Acts 18:24-28)

"He began to speak boldly in the synagogue; but when Priscilla and Aquila heard him, they took him aside and explained to him the Way [of God] more accurately."

As the young church began to grow, more and more people were interested in hearing the Good News, and those who heard it began sharing what they had heard with others, who in turn became interested. In this passage we read of Apollos who had been sharing with others, to great effect, what he had learned. As he was sharing in the synagogue, two of St. Paul's disciples saw that he did not know everything that was being taught by St. Paul and the other apostles. When he was finished they took him aside and taught him all they knew. This story is a good example for us. Many times we are afraid to share our faith with others, because we feel that we do not know enough about it. But Jesus calls us to share what we do know and all that we have experienced in him. Each of us has a special relationship with the Lord. Each of us has been touched and healed by God in a special way. We are called to share our stories with others. As we continue to live and share our faith we will learn more, but sharing what we know now is enough. Just bringing Jesus to others in our limited way allows Jesus to touch the hearts of others and begin to change their lives.

15

GREATER THINGS THAN THESE WILL YOU DO

Our Lord continues to remind us that if we wish to grow in our relationship with him, we must be servants to all. Jesus calls us into service in very different and unique ways. He asks that we remain open to his call into his service. He tells us that as we answer his call he will provide every gift and grace that we need for the task.

PRAYER

Lord, open our hearts and minds to hear you as you call us to be servants to each other. Make us useable and use us in ministry to you. Build up our trust in you so we come to know that you will provide every gift and grace that we need in saying yes to your call.

Were Not Our Hearts Burning!

(Leviticus 25:8-17)

"Do not deal unfairly, then; but stand in fear of your God."

Being shrewd in business is a quality that is much admired in our society. Getting a "good deal," even at the expense of someone else, is applauded. Our Lord reminds us that this should not be the way for us. He reminds us that we are all connected. We are all children of God and as such, members of one family. He admonishes us to treat each other with respect and dignity, to treat each other with fairness and compassion. He tells us that it is the virtue of humility that he desires. He asks us to reflect on the fairness and mercy with which he treats us. Let us aspire to make Jesus our example. He humbled himself and laid down his life for us. He treated all people with respect and dignity. He always put the welfare of others before his own. By standing in opposition to many of the practices of his society, he was able to change the world. We are called to be part of that change. We are called to put fairness and compassion ahead of our own interests. In doing so, our lives will be more complete and we will have a hand in changing the world and bringing to fruition the kingdom of God on earth.

Greater Things Than These Will You Do

(John 13:1-15)

"If I, therefore, the master and teacher, have washed your feet, you
ought to wash one another's feet."

The apostles were stunned when Jesus began washing their feet. They
had already come to realize that Jesus was the Messiah. They knew him
as their master and teacher, and yet here was Jesus washing their feet.
Jesus' action certainly brought home the point, both to his disciples
and to us, that God's kingdom is about love and service. It is not about
might and power as we might define those terms. The might and power
of God are made manifest in our service to one another. Our Lord calls
us to follow the example he gave us. He calls us to willingly serve one
another. He calls us to strip away from ourselves the pride that keeps
us from being good servants. He calls us to make manifest the power,
might, and glory of God through the love and service that we extend
to all of our brothers and sisters. Let us pray for the gift of humility,
that we can more clearly hear our Lord's call to service. Let us pray that
we begin to see more clearly the plan of God to win his people over to
himself through love and service, and that we do our part to further the
plan of God on earth.

Were Not Our Hearts Burning!

(Isaiah 50:4-9)

"The Lord has given me a well trained tongue, that I might know how to speak to the weary a word that will rouse them. Morning after morning he opens my ear that I may hear; and I have not rebelled, have not turned back."

When we are open to the prompting of the Lord in our lives, he will use us in many different ways. He will give us the gifts we need to build up his people, especially those who are downtrodden and need encouragement and faith. He will give us the strength to comfort those who are sorrowful. Through the power of the Holy Spirit, he will give us the words we need in any situation. It is not the easiest thing for us to be always open to the Word of God. To be always open requires sacrifice. It requires determination and strength. When we open our hearts to the Word of the Lord, we may not always be popular or well received. As compassionate as Jesus was, he was not always well received. But as he continued to hear and then speak the Word of God, so must we. As he continued to champion the cause for peace and justice for all people, so must we. As he continued to comfort and console those in distress, so must we. Our God has chosen to work through willing servants to strengthen and comfort his people. He calls us to be open to him so that we may be his instruments in sharing his love and peace with all who are longing for love and comfort in their lives. Let us open our hearts to share the great love of God, which he continues to pour out on our world.

Greater Things Than These Will You Do

(John 14:7-14)

"Amen, amen, I say to you, whoever believes in me will do the works that I do, and will do greater ones than these, because I am going to the Father."

It pleases the Lord to vest his strength and power in those who believe in him. Jesus tells us that those who believe and open their lives to him will be given the power of the Holy Spirit to bring the healing, peace, and joy of Christ to God's people, just as Jesus did when he was ministering on earth. Jesus reminds us that it is our lives, our hearts, and our hands that will be used by him in the building of the kingdom of God. He tells us that for those who believe, nothing will be impossible in him. He will make us worthy. He will provide us with the gifts and the strength that we need to carry out his plan. He simply calls us to believe. He calls us to build our faith and trust in him through prayer and through a new boldness in his name. He calls us to step out in faith, knowing that he will provide all that we need. He calls us to put on his heart and mind, remembering the love that he has for his people, and to live our lives in love and compassion for all of our brothers and sisters. We know that we need the healing, peace, and joy of Christ in our world. Jesus tells us that it is our faith in him that will make that happen. We must come to realize that each of us has tremendous power in Jesus' name.

Were Not Our Hearts Burning!

(Matthew 5:38-42)

"Give to the one who asks of you, and do not turn your back on the one who wants to borrow."

A well-accepted saying in our society is that only the strong survive. We are taught from an early age to look out for number one. We see in our society that there is never too much when it comes to wealth, leisure, and comfort. Yet, here is Jesus telling us that we must look out for each other. We must never turn our backs on those in need. We are to refuse no one who asks for our help. This might be an area of our spiritual growth that should be examined and changes made. Jesus reminds us that we are all part of the same body. We are all created in the image of God. We are all brothers and sisters in Christ. Jesus reminds us that each of us has been given gifts that must be shared with others. He admonishes us not to hoard any gift we have been given, whether it be material wealth, talent, or time. He explains that everything we have been given should be used to build the kingdom of God on earth. This passage may be a hard lesson for us, but we are called to examine our lives and share with others all that we have been so graciously given.

Greater Things Than These Will You Do

(Exodus 3:1-12)

"But Moses said to God, 'Who am I that I should go to Pharaoh and
lead the Israelites out of Egypt?'"

As we read the stories of the prophets and others whom our Lord has
used as instruments, we notice that all of them had questions about
their worthiness to serve the Lord. All had doubts as to their suitability
to perform the tasks to which they were called. In this passage, Moses
expresses those feelings to the Lord. He cannot even fathom the idea
that he will be able to complete the work the Lord has called him to do.
Even after the Lord reassures him, he is still fearful and doubtful about
his ability to carry out the work of the Lord. After all, Moses is just an
ordinary person. Before Moses was called by the Lord, he had no special
talents. In fact, he had been a sinner who had even killed another man.
Yet, the power of God was made manifest through him. We are called to
take courage from the lives of those whom the Lord has used throughout our salvation history. We know that we, too, are sinners. We, too,
are unworthy. We, too, are just ordinary people with limited skills and
talents. Yet, if we are open to the Lord, he will give us the gifts we need,
and his power will be made manifest through us.

Were Not Our Hearts Burning!

(Luke 19:11-28)

"I tell you, to everyone who has, more will be given, but from the one who has not, even what he has will be taken away."

This passage recounts the very familiar parable of the ten gold coins. We read that only two of the servants invested what they had been given so they could return more to the king. The third servant was afraid and did nothing. What little he had left was taken away. This may seem harsh to us. Jesus was teaching that we have all received gifts from God, and each of us is called to use and develop those gifts for the building and betterment of the kingdom of God. Each of us is called to contribute to the best of our ability. We know that the will and the plan of our God for our world will be fulfilled. It will be fulfilled with our involvement or without it. Our Lord desires that his will be accomplished with our involvement. He wants us to be involved and committed to his plan. We are reminded, however, that if we do not choose to be part of his plan, the gifts he has given us that lie dormant within us, will be given to those who strive to bring about God's plan for our world. Let us pray for the grace and the courage to use all of the gifts the Lord has given us for the building of the kingdom of God.

Greater Things Than These Will You Do

(Matthew 9:35–10:15)

"Without cost you have received; without cost you are to give."

Everything we have is a gift from God. All that we have been able to accomplish in our lives is by the grace of God. All of our talents, all of our abilities come from God. Without his divine providence we could not even take a breath. Jesus reminds us of this truth. He reminds us that we have been greatly blessed by God. He also reminds us that as the Lord has given to us, we must give to others. This command of Jesus can be a difficult one for us. In our human weakness, we can easily become very possessive of the talents and the material goods with which we have been blessed. We can easily become intoxicated by the successes we have been able to attain. We can become stingy and begin to hoard the gifts that the Lord has so graciously provided us. Accomplishments, and all that we have acquired can take the majority of our effort, leaving little time or energy to follow the Lord. Let us pray for the courage to trust in God, trusting him with even those things of which we are most possessive. Let us pray for the grace to be able to give to others as the Lord has given to us.

Were Not Our Hearts Burning!

(1 Corinthians 12:4-11)

"To each individual the manifestation of the Spirit is given for some benefit."

St. Paul reminds us that we, the followers of Christ, are the church. Each of us has a role to play in the body of Christ. Each of us has received a calling from God to build his church on earth. Too often, we think of the church as the building where we attend services. Too often, we think that it is up to our pastors to build the church, that if there are any gifts of the Spirit, they would be made manifest only in our ordained clergy. We can attend "church" and be satisfied that we are doing all that we can to lead a good spiritual life. St. Paul tells us that this is not the case. He reminds us that each of us has gifts. Each of us is a manifestation of the Spirit for the benefit of the church. He calls us to be open to every gift of the Holy Spirit. He admonishes us that if we are not open to the gifts the Holy Spirit brings, we not only harm ourselves, but harm the larger church as well. Let us strive to learn more about the gift of the Holy Spirit and all that he brings to us and to the church. Let us look for ways in which the Holy Spirit might use us for the benefit of the church. Finally, let us remember that each of us is a member of the body of Christ. We are the church. Thanks be to God!

Greater Things Than These Will You Do

(Luke 1:39-45)

"During those days Mary set out and traveled to the hill country in haste to a town of Judah, where she entered the house of Zechariah and greeted Elizabeth."

Mary had just been told that she was to be the mother of the Savior of the world. She was blessed above all women. Yet, here she was setting out on a long trip to be of service to her cousin Elizabeth, who would soon give birth to John the Baptist. Instead of being filled with pride and self-importance, Mary put on the heart of a servant and went to the aid of her cousin. Mary is truly an example for us. In putting on the heart of a servant, Mary foreshadowed the path that her Son would take in his life. Jesus, too, would come to us as a servant instead of a king. His life would be spent in service to the forgotten and the broken, to men and women from all classes and walks of life. Each of us is also called to put on the heart of a servant. We are called to serve the forgotten and the broken, and men and women from all classes and walks of life. Let us reflect on the example of Mary. We ask God for the grace and strength to follow her example of service, her example of humility before the majestic presence of our God.

Were Not Our Hearts Burning!

(Acts 6:1-7)

"Brothers, select from among you seven reputable men, filled with
the Spirit and wisdom, whom we shall appoint to this task, whereas
we shall devote ourselves to prayer and to the ministry of the word."

There are and must be different ministries to promote growth in the
church. There is not one person, or even one class of people, who can or
should try to minister in all areas of the church and community life. Our
pastors, priests, and religious leaders have the ministry of the apostles.
Like the apostles, they are called to devote their lives to prayer and the
ministry of word and sacrament. There are ministries for the laity as well.
The church will suffer if the laity is not involved in its life and ministry.
Each of us, as members of the church, must define and discern, with the
guidance of the Holy Spirit, the ministry to which we are called. Like
the apostles and disciples who were called into ministry, we must pray
to be filled with the Holy Spirit and wisdom so that we can discern and
then fulfill the call we receive in Christ Jesus.

16

BEAR FRUIT
THAT WILL LAST

Our God continues to call us into a closer relationship with himself. He continues to call us to strive for holiness. It is in striving for holiness that we grow in our spiritual lives. It is in striving for holiness that we come closer to God and to the reward of eternal life offered in Jesus' name to all who faithfully follow him.

PRAYER

Lord, help us to know you and to experience you more fully in our lives. Open our hearts and minds to your guidance as you teach us to grow in holiness. Give us a strong love for your laws. Help us to understand that it is in striving to be holy that we attain happiness and peace in this life, as well as confidence in the hope of eternal life where we will be with you forever.

Were Not Our Hearts Burning!

(Matthew 6:19-23)

"For where your treasure is, there also will your heart be."

During his life on earth, Jesus talked many times about priorities. He talked many times about keeping our focus on God. He talked many times about focusing our attention on heaven, keeping our minds on the things that are above, rather than those of earth. Jesus directs our thoughts to building up our spiritual lives and the importance of concentrating our efforts on receiving and sharing the grace of God in our lives. With all of the temptations that exist in the world and with the strong secular pull of our society, it is easy for us to lose focus on the important priorities of which Jesus speaks. It is easy to become trapped into striving for those things that are important to the world, but of no importance to our ultimate goal of eternal life. Jesus talked so much about priorities because it is so easy for us to get them confused. As we strive to get our priorities in order, let us pray to the Lord for his help and guidance. Let us open our lives to the prompting and teaching of the Holy Spirit, that we might see what is truly important and concentrate our efforts on those things alone.

Bear Fruit That Will Last

(Luke 2:22-40)

"When they had fulfilled all the prescriptions of the law of the Lord,
they returned to Galilee, to their own town of Nazareth."

In the presentation of Jesus to the Father, we become aware of our own obligation to serve the Lord. Mary and Joseph lived a holy life in the knowledge of their dependence on God. They lived fully in the law of Moses, as did Jesus. In this passage we read that they fulfilled all the law commanded, and in presenting Jesus to the Father were blessed with God's grace. In his submission to the will of God and in the grace given to Mary and Joseph, Jesus grew in wisdom and grace. We, too, must realize that we belong to the Lord. We, too, are called to dedicate our lives to God. When we dedicate our lives and our wills to God, we will receive his grace and blessing in our lives. We will grow in confidence and wisdom. We will grow in the grace of God through the power of the Holy Spirit. As we contemplate the presentation of Jesus, let us pray for the grace and courage to dedicate our lives fully to the Lord, and that in following his will for our lives we will grow in holiness and wisdom.

Were Not Our Hearts Burning!

(Hosea 2:16-25)

"So I will allure her; I will lead her into the desert and speak to her heart."

The Lord is continually calling us to examine our lives and come closer to him. Sometimes, it is easier for us to hear the Lord better when we slow down a little bit and step back from the hustle and bustle of our lives. It is in that slowing down, that quietness of spirit, that the Lord can truly speak to our hearts. Jesus himself went into the desert after he was baptized to clear his mind of the many responsibilities that life always presents. He needed time to really hear God the Father speak to his heart. We know that when he had taken that time, he emerged much stronger and with a set plan for his public ministry. He was in tune with God's plan for his life. We, too, are called to let the Lord lead us into that quiet place where he can speak to our hearts. When God speaks to our hearts, we are built stronger in faith and hope. We are given the strength to successfully combat the temptations of our lives. We become more open to the plan of God for our lives. We can better experience the love, peace, and joy of our God. Lord, lead us to your quiet place! Speak to our hearts!

Bear Fruit That Will Last

(Isaiah 58:9-14)

"If you remove from your midst oppression, false accusation and malicious speech; if you bestow your bread on the hungry and satisfy the afflicted; then light shall rise for you in the darkness, and the gloom shall become for you like midday; then the Lord will guide you always and give you plenty even on the parched land."

The prophet Isaiah speaks this word of the Lord, which guides us to the holiness to which we are called. The Lord calls us to change our lives. He calls us to forsake the way the world looks at life, and embrace the way he looks at life. He calls us to a higher level of love, a higher level of humility. In calling us to this higher level of holiness, he promises his help. He promises a new joy in our lives. He promises us that we will live in his light. There will be no more darkness in our souls. He promises to guide us and provide for our needs, even amidst the trial and sorrow of the world. Let these words of God, spoken through Isaiah, guide us as we examine our lives. Let us open our lives to the changing power of God's grace that we may come to the new level of holiness to which we are continually being called.

Were Not Our Hearts Burning!

(Matthew 5:43-48)

"So be perfect, just as your heavenly Father is perfect."

As Christian men and women we are called to a higher standard. We are called to live lives of example and to strive for perfection. Jesus reminds us that it is not difficult to do only what is easy, to love only those who agree with us, to love those who are friends and family. He says that we must do more. We must go all the way in striving to be perfect as the Father is perfect. There is no halfway with God. Even though it is not easy to love those who are our enemies, those who may have wronged us in the past or those who are unkind to us, that is exactly what Jesus calls us to do. We have only to look at the Lord's unconditional love for us as an example of how we should love others. Even though we continually fall short in our efforts to achieve the perfection to which we are called, our Lord does not abandon us. He continues to love us. He continues to forgive us. He continues to help us begin again. That is the example we should strive to emulate in our dealings with others. If God continues to forgive and love us, can we not try to do the same in our relationships with those who fall short in their dealings with us? Every person has been created in the image of God. Let us strive to love every person as our God loves us.

Bear Fruit That Will Last

(1 Timothy 4:12-16)

"Attend to yourself and to your teaching; persevere in both tasks, for
by doing so you will save both yourself and those who
listen to you."

We know that we have been called to be a light to others. We are called to
lead the way to the Lord, who through his gift of faith to us has changed
our lives, and through his love and mercy has touched our hearts. We
are called to lead others to the Lord by both word and action. St. Paul
reminds us that we must persevere in this calling, but he also reminds
us that we must continue to nurture our own faith and grow in holiness,
coming always closer to the Lord. It is important for our own salvation
that we always take care to be attentive to our own gift of faith, and never
allow our own light to grow dim. St. Paul explains that if we grow in
our own faith, and if we keep the light of the Lord shining brightly in
ourselves, we will be more effective in leading others to the Lord, while
remaining alive in the grace and love of God. As we strive for the prize
of eternal life, others will be able to see in us the saving power of God
at work. Praise you, Lord!

Were Not Our Hearts Burning!

(1 Samuel 24:1-23)

"The Lord will be the judge; he will decide between me and you."

Saul was jealous of David because he was to take Saul's place as king of Israel. It had been Saul's intention to kill David, but David found and could have easily killed Saul first. David's men certainly thought he should do so, for they knew that David had become Saul's enemy. It would have been easy for David to listen to his men, and he would have had no problem justifying his action to the people of Israel. Yet, David did Saul no harm. He left it for God to judge between them. Jesus has told us throughout the New Testament that we should not judge others. He tells us that God is the only true Judge. Jesus commands us to love our enemies and do them no harm, to leave justice to the Lord. David did so and was blessed by God. It could not have been easy for him, but he surrendered his will in this matter to the Lord. We, too, must surrender to God any hatred or vengeance we carry in our hearts. When we surrender our will to the Lord, when we surrender our anger and hatred to him, he will heal and bless us. He will bring his peace into our lives.

Bear Fruit That Will Last

(Acts 20:28-38)

"So be vigilant and remember that for three years, night and day, I unceasingly admonished each of you with tears."

St. Paul reminds us that living a good Christian life takes courage. There will always be some who will try to lead us away from the truth. There may be some from among our own, who, in good conscience, try to lead us from the true way of the Lord. St. Paul tells us that we know the truth. We have been steeped in the truth through the Word of God in Scripture, and through the teaching of the church and our pastors. We are told that we must hold strongly to that truth and to help each other in the struggles we face as we strive to live out our faith in Jesus. Our Lord calls us to a deeper knowledge of our faith, a deeper knowledge of his way for us, so that we cannot be easily led astray. Just as St. Paul worked unceasingly on behalf of his flock, he calls us to work unceasingly as we strive to live the holy lives to which we are called. Our faith can never be just a part of our lives. Our faith must be our life. We must rely on the strong foundation of faith we have in Jesus so that we will remain in his truth and light. He is our Rock. He is our Fortress. There is no one else who compares with him.

Were Not Our Hearts Burning!

(Mark 3:1-6)

"Looking around at them with anger and grieved at their hardness of heart, he said to the man, 'Stretch out your hand.'"

The first law of God is love. All of the commandments and teachings of the Lord revolve around love of God and neighbor. Many times, Jesus was confronted with people's hardness of heart, those who thought the law was more important than love of neighbor. In this passage we read that Jesus was grieved by the people's lack of understanding. We are called to learn this lesson. We, too, can become confused about the importance of laws and rules. Jesus has always said that his commandments and laws are very important. He told us that he did not come to abolish even one law. He did, however, come to bring understanding to the law. He teaches that all of his commandments, all of his laws, will lead us to love to keep us ever mindful of our call to be servants of God and each other. We are called to examine our understanding of God's laws as they relate to love. We are called to keep all of God's commandments and to use the commands and teachings of Jesus to lead us to a higher love of both God and each other.

Bear Fruit That Will Last

(Mark 4:1-20)

"They are the people who hear the word, but worldly anxiety, the lure of riches, and the craving for other things intrude and choke the word, and it bears no fruit."

The demands of the life that we lead are formidable. Time constraints, stress, and anxiety are all a major part of the society in which we live. The chase for a better life can easily take over our lives. The balance between a comfortable life and a good spiritual life can become skewed away from the path of God. Jesus is aware of the difficulties we face. He admonishes us that receiving the Word of God is only the first step in living a holy life. We must make sure that the Word we receive has a chance to grow and become a way of life for us. Jesus warns that there are many ways we can lose the power of his Word for our lives. Jesus reminds us that the choices we make affect the power of the Word that we have received. We must not allow the demands of the world to get in the way of nurturing the Word of God. We must make time for the Word to grow. We must find places that the Word can be nourished, such as our churches and being among other believers. Jesus will always be there to help us. He will always bless us with the grace of understanding if we strive to make the right choices, so that his Word will grow and bear fruit in our lives.

Were Not Our Hearts Burning!

(Mark 7:14-23)

"All these evils come from within and they defile."

All of God's creation is beautiful. Everything that has been created by our God is a manifestation of his love and kindness, his glory and majesty. In this passage, Jesus reminds the crowd that evil does not come from external things, but comes from within the heart of a person. He tells them that they can control evil by controlling themselves. It is so much easier to put the blame on external things for our own shortcomings and failures. We can convince ourselves that the sins we commit are not really our fault, but the fault of external forces that are beyond our control. Jesus calls us to understand that it is ourselves that we must master. It is our own hearts and minds that we must control. He calls us to a responsibility for our own thoughts, our own actions, our own sins. He calls us to examine our own lives to see if we are guilty of blaming other people or things for actions or thoughts that should be under our own control. Jesus understands that this world is difficult. He understands that we are sinners. He tells us that it is only in taking responsibility for ourselves that we can truly live in the grace and light of God.

Bear Fruit That Will Last

(Mark 1:14-15)

"Repent, and believe in the gospel."

Such a simple statement, and yet it is sometimes so difficult for us to do. It is important for us to understand the basics of what Jesus is asking of us. We have heard the answer from the mouth of Jesus himself. He calls us to repentance and then to believe in the truth that he proclaims. All of us are constantly seeking truth. We are looking for those people and those things in which to place our trust. Jesus is the answer for us. We can believe in him and all he has taught us. We can believe in the good news of salvation. We can believe in the presence of the kingdom of God. Jesus tells us that as we come to believe more strongly in the gospel, we must live it every day in our lives. As we come to believe in the gospel, we will be able to do no less than live it powerfully and proclaim it joyfully. Jesus teaches us that we begin that journey of total belief in repentance. We begin that journey by forsaking the wisdom of the world and embracing the wisdom of the Lord. Jesus calls us to begin today in that journey to a deeper belief in him. Indeed it is a simple statement, but if we heed the Lord we will be changed forever.

Were Not Our Hearts Burning!

(John 10:1-10)

"So Jesus said again, 'Amen, amen, I say to you, I am the gate for the sheep.'"

Jesus makes very clear to us that he is the only way to the Father. He is the only way for us to reach our goal of eternal life. He is not only the true Shepherd, but also the Gate. Every person must enter through him. He knows us, and as we open our hearts and minds to him we begin to recognize the voice of the Shepherd. As we open our hearts to him, he leads us on the path we must follow to find peace and joy in our lives. Jesus calls us to recognize his voice by staying close to him in prayer and by following his teachings and commandments. He calls us to recognize his voice by remaining faithful to our calling and by being fed and strengthened in our faith communities. As we reflect on the importance of Jesus' words, let us begin to concentrate our efforts on hearing the Lord as our Shepherd. Let us concentrate on filtering out those voices, which would lead us away from the Lord. Let us begin to understand that Jesus is the only Gate for us, that in him we have salvation and that there is no other way by which we might reach our goal of heaven.

Bear Fruit That Will Last

(John 15:1-8)

"You are already pruned because of the word that I spoke to you."

Jesus reminds us that we must continue to grow in our faith and in our relationship with him. It is only in our striving to grow that we become strong. It is only in striving to grow that we remain strong branches on the Vine, which is Christ. Jesus tells us that our growth depends on being pruned, as well as being nurtured. The pruning that we undergo helps to make us grow and bear an abundance of fruit. Our Lord explains that we must be open to being pruned so that we can bear more and better fruit. Following the way of the Lord by adhering to his laws is one of the main ways in which we are pruned by the Father. If we do not obey his laws, we will surely wither on the vine, but when we allow the law of God to rule our hearts and our lives, we gain strength and bear good fruit. We are made strong and happy in the Lord. We are fully nourished and nurtured as branches on the Vine. Let us be strong in our commitment to follow the laws of God in our lives, that we may remain always strong branches on the Vine that is Christ.

Were Not Our Hearts Burning!

(Matthew 7:21-29)

"Not everyone who says to me, 'Lord, Lord,' will enter the kingdom of heaven, but only the one who does the will of my Father in heaven."

Actions speak louder than words, and Jesus reminds us it is our actions and not just our words that are pleasing to him and will secure for us the reward for which we strive. Jesus calls us to put our faith in him into action. We are called to live out that which we proclaim. We know all too well that there are many who talk a good game, who say all the right things, but their actions do not bear out the words they speak. We know from experience that this hurts not only those people themselves, but affects others who are turned off by their hypocrisy. Many might turn away from the Lord because of the hypocrisy of a few. The Lord calls us to examine our own lives. He calls us to make sure that we are not saying one thing while living another. He calls us to a life lived in faith, a life lived in the love we proclaim. He assures us that living boldly in him will bring peace and joy to our own lives, as well as set a good example for others who are seeking the Lord in their lives. Let us pray for the grace to live every day the faith that we proclaim.

Bear Fruit That Will Last

(Matthew 9:14-17)

"People do not put new wine into old wineskins. Otherwise the
skins burst, the wine spills out, and the skins are ruined."

Our Lord calls us to be constantly renewed in our faith. He calls us to
continual repentance and renewal through his most gracious forgiveness
and mercy. He calls us to continually strive for a life of holiness, a life of
perfection. Our human weakness and propensity to sin can keep us from
that life of holiness. Jesus compares those souls who wallow in sin and
weakness to old wineskins. If we do not renew our souls through penance
and reconciliation with him, our souls will be like those old wineskins,
unable to perceive and contain the many blessings and graces that God
showers upon us. Our souls will not be able to contain all that the Lord
wants us to have, and soon we will find ourselves further and further
away from the Lord and the life to which he calls us. It is through a life
of continual repentance and renewal that our souls are made strong, that
we are able to contain all the graces that the Lord showers upon us. It is
through constant renewal that we grow in love, that we attain the peace
and joy for which we search, and that we are able to live more closely
that life of holiness to which we are called in Christ.

Were Not Our Hearts Burning!

(Matthew 13:54-58)

"Is he not the carpenter's son?"

Some of the people who knew Jesus best, both as a child and as a young man, were able to get the least out of his teaching and the mighty works he continued to perform throughout the region. They thought they knew Jesus and were unwilling to see him in the new power of his baptism. They were unwilling to see the Holy Spirit working so powerfully through him. They were unwilling to see the Son of God revealed in this common man who had grown up in their midst. In our human weakness and in our tendency to judge, we often fail to recognize the teaching and power of Jesus in the people around us. We are quick to judge people, both by their pasts and what others say about them. We judge people because we think we know them. We may find that we judge people for many other reasons, and thereby miss many blessings that could be ours through the efforts of others. Jesus cautions us to refrain from judging others. He reminds us that he uses many people in many different ways to accomplish his plan, and urges us to be open to all of the people around us, and to try to see him in everyone we know and everyone we meet. The power and the teaching of Jesus is made manifest everywhere. He calls us to be open to all of the possibilities.

Bear Fruit That Will Last

(Exodus 24:3-11)

"When Moses came to the people and related all the words and ordinances of the Lord, they all answered with one voice, 'We will do everything that the Lord has told us.'"

In this passage the people of Israel accept the ordinances of the Lord. They had just seen the glory of God descend upon them and were eager to believe and follow the way of the Lord. We know that as the trials and temptations of life began to tear people away from the euphoria they had experienced and back to the realities of life on this earth, they found it much more difficult to keep the promises they had made. As they went back on their promises, they found themselves further and further away from the Lord. Our intentions are always good. We always start out strong in our resolve to follow the teachings and commandments of God. As we are confronted by the realities of life, however, we find it much more difficult to live the lives we want to live. Our God calls us to keep in the forefront the promises we have made by staying close to him in his Word in Scripture and in his sacraments. He tells us that the closer we stay to him, the easier it will be for us to keep our promises to him as he continues to bless and strengthen us.

Were Not Our Hearts Burning!

(Luke 7:31-35)

"For John the Baptist came neither eating food nor drinking wine,
and you said, 'He is possessed by a demon.' The Son of Man came
eating and drinking and you said, 'Look he is a glutton and a
drunkard, a friend of tax collectors and sinners.'"

Many of the people in Jesus' time were entrenched in their religious ways.
They were invested in the way their religion was practiced and had no
desire to change their lives. Because of this, they were slow to understand
the new way of life that Jesus brought to the world. They were not open
to a new relationship with God. Therefore, they found ways to disparage
Jesus and his new teachings. In our lives we sometimes fall into that
same trap. We become comfortable in our relationship with God and
are slow to open our hearts to a new kind of relationship with him. Our
Lord constantly calls to partake in a fuller and closer relationship with
him. He constantly calls us to broaden our relationship with him. He asks
that we not become so complacent in our relationship with him that we
refuse to grow in his life and love. He tells us that he has so much more
for us, and not to sell ourselves short. Our God is mighty and awesome.
Let us experience him in every way that we can.

Bear Fruit That Will Last

(James 3:16–4:3)

"For where jealousy and selfish ambition exist, there is disorder and every foul practice."

St. James admonishes us to put away all jealousy and ambition. He says that to be happy in this life we must keep our priorities straight and focus on those things that are the most important for us. He confirms what we already know, both in our lives and in our world, that jealousy and ambition lead only to heartache. He says that the world will tear itself apart if jealousy and blind ambition continue to be fostered. If jealousy and ambition take root in our lives, the happiness and peace that we have in our faith will rot away. Jesus confirms what St. James tells us, when he reminds us that we must be humble servants to all. We must never strive to be the greatest. In taking up the servant's role, rather than putting on jealousy or ambition, we can help our Lord establish his kingdom. We can bring his peace and love to a world much in need of his presence.

Were Not Our Hearts Burning!

(Luke 17:7-10)

"When you have done all you have been commanded, say, 'We are unprofitable servants; we have done what we were obliged to do.'"

St. Paul told us that we have nothing to boast of in ourselves. Everything we have is a gift from God. In this passage, Jesus confirms what St. Paul said. All of us want to bask in the good things we do. All of us want credit for hard work done. All of us want to be told that we have done a good job. And yet, here is Jesus telling us that all we do for the Father is only what is expected. Jesus teaches that we will find peace and happiness in doing the will of God. We need no further praise. Our reward comes in praising and honoring the Father in all that we do. Jesus explains that we will never go wanting in our relationship with God. He calls us to trust in the Father for all that we need, always confident that the Lord will provide for us. He reminds us that God loves us so much that he will give us every good thing. Let us pray that we find our happiness and peace in living our lives for the Lord. Let us pray that we come to trust the Lord in all things.

Bear Fruit That Will Last

(Luke 21:29-33)

"Heaven and earth will pass away, but my words will not pass away."

Our lives continually change. We know that there are seasons for everything. It seems that in the hectic world in which we live, change is a way of life. We are forever moving around, or entering new phases in our lives. Certainly, change will always be a part of our lives on earth. In fact, the Lord himself is continually calling us to change our ways, to forsake sin, and to always keep moving closer to him. He is constantly calling us to renewal. He wants us to know that in the midst of all this change, he is our Rock. He is our one constant, no matter what other changes we are going through. The power of his Word is forever. No matter what is left behind, no matter what lies ahead, we can always count on the constancy of his Word to guide us. As we reflect on our busy and changing lives, we pray that we are ever mindful of the constancy of God's Word in our lives. We pray that we always be able to recognize that the Lord is our Rock, especially in times of change and confusion. Let us know that our God will always be there for us.

Were Not Our Hearts Burning!

(1 Samuel 3:1-10)

"Samuel answered, 'Speak, for your servant is listening.'"

The Lord constantly calls us to reach new heights in our spiritual growth. He calls us always to hear his voice as we negotiate the pitfalls of our earthly lives. This passage relates the first time that Samuel heard the Lord. At first, he is unfamiliar with the voice of the Lord. He does not recognize the way the Lord wants to lead him. As he begins to become familiar with the Lord's voice in his life, the Lord is able to guide and use him. Many times in our lives we fail to recognize the voice of the Lord. Sometimes, we may even be intentionally deaf to him. We may be afraid that the Lord will call us to some service for which we are not prepared. It may be that we just don't want to change our lives. Our Lord tells us that we will only be truly happy in our lives when we hear and heed his voice. Our God tells us that when we come humbly before him, with our hearts and minds open to him, we cannot fail to recognize his voice. Let us reflect on our lives to make sure that we are open to hearing the Word of God, even if hearing him brings discomfort or change to our lives.

Bear Fruit That Will Last

(Mark 3:1-6)

"They watched him closely to see if he would cure him on the sabbath, so that they might accuse him."

When we read of the obstinance of the scribes and Pharisees to the coming of the Messiah, we wonder how they could be so blind. We wonder how they could fail to see the majesty and glory of Jesus. Here we have another example of the blindness of some people concerning Jesus. They were totally blinded to his compassion and his mighty healing power. They looked at this miracle only as a way to trap him and thus accuse him of crimes against the faith. Jesus reminds us that there may be areas in our own lives in which we are blind to his love and care. There may be areas of our lives that we try to keep hidden from him. Because of our blindness, we fail to see the glory and majesty of God as we should. We fail to fully experience his love. Our Lord asks us to reflect on the areas of our lives in which we might be blind to him. He asks that we lay that blindness at his feet so that he may heal us and bring us more fully into his light and love.

Were Not Our Hearts Burning!

(2 Samuel 6:12-23)

"Then David, girt with linen apron, came dancing before the Lord
with abandon, as he and all the Israelites were bringing up the ark of
the Lord with shouts of joy and to the sound of the horn."

David was the king of the whole of Israel. He was the most powerful
man in the kingdom, and yet we read that he humbled himself before
the Lord, dancing with abandon as the ark of the Lord was brought into
Jerusalem. He did not care what anyone thought about him. He knew
that before he was the king he was a child of God, and his God was more
important than anything on earth. The humility of David before the
Lord should be an example for us. Too many times in our lives we try
to keep our spiritual and earthly lives separate. We try to separate our
spiritual beliefs from our world beliefs. Our secular society encourages
this type of separation, trying to keep anything that is even remotely
religious out of the secular arena. We must not fall into this trap. We
must remember that before anything else in our lives we are children
of God. God and our spiritual growth must always come first. With the
help of God's grace, we must come to realize that God wants us to surrender our whole selves to him. In return, he promises to be with us
always and bless us abundantly.

Bear Fruit That Will Last

(Mark 4:21-25)

"He also told them, 'Be careful what you hear.'"

Jesus reminds us that he alone is the Way, and the Truth, and the Life. His Word is our truth, and he cautions us to be careful to hear only his truth. We live in the information age. With the Internet and the many other ways by which we receive information, there is a mountain of information available, and some of it is not the truth. There are many who bash our Christian way of life and try to persuade Christian people to abandon their faith. There are theories about how our world came into being that dismiss God as Creator of the world. We are bombarded with information on every subject including God, church, and faith. Jesus reminds us that his teachings and commandments encompass all truth. He calls us to hear and then live his truth. As we hear and live his truth, we become examples for others. Let us pray for God's gift of wisdom and discernment that we might always know his truth, and then for courage that we may live out his truth in our lives.

Were Not Our Hearts Burning!

(Hosea 6:1-6)

"He will come to us like the rain, like spring rain which waters
the earth."

The prophet Hosea helps us lift a prayer to the Lord. It is a beautiful prayer, in which we ask the Lord to help us know him, to understand more fully the way in which he guides our lives, and a prayer to affirm that we will return to him. The vision of Hosea concerning how the Lord will help us includes the beautiful image of spring rain. The rain will wash us clean. It will refresh us. But a spring rain connotes even more. Spring rain helps everything it touches grow. The spring rain of God's love will help build our faith. It will softly nurture the many gifts that he has given us. It will renew our spirits and our lives. Our Lord will forever be the source of our growth and renewal. Let us open our hearts to the spring rain of God's love. Let us pray that we will be renewed in the Lord. Let us pray that we will be strengthened in the Lord. Let us pray that this will be a time of real growth as we let the love of God rain down upon us.

Bear Fruit That Will Last

(John 11:45-57)

"If we leave him alone, all will believe in him, and the Romans will
come and take both our land and our nation."

In this passage we are again confronted with the fact that some were never
to believe in Jesus. Their hearts and minds were closed because of other
considerations. They had power and would do nothing to jeopardize
what they had. Their decision was that Jesus must die, rather than risk
any change to their way of life. Our Lord asks that we examine our own
lives. He asks us if there are considerations in our lives that keep us from
being fully open to him. He asks us if the material things we own, or the
lifestyles we choose, get in the way of our following him more closely.
We can easily see the mistakes the Jewish leaders made. Our Lord asks
us if we can as easily see the mistakes of our own lives and our failure
to surrender our lives to him. Let us be honest with ourselves. Let us
offer our weaknesses to the Lord that he may heal us. Let us pray that
in that healing we will find the courage to strengthen our commitment
to love and follow him.

Were Not Our Hearts Burning!

(John 6:30-35)

"Jesus said to them, 'I am the bread of life; whoever comes to me will never hunger, and whoever believes in me will never thirst.'"

Jesus had just fed the multitudes by the miracle of the multiplication of the loaves and fishes. Now they were amazed to hear Jesus say that if they continued to believe in him they would never be hungry or thirsty again. The people were thinking in terms of their bodily needs, but Jesus was talking in terms of their spiritual needs. They misinterpreted what Jesus was saying. Jesus continues to offer us complete spiritual nourishment. He calls us to ever-stronger faith in him, and in that faith he promises that we will live rich and full lives. We are cautioned against misinterpreting Jesus as did the crowd in this passage. We are called to understand the importance of our spiritual sustenance and understand that our souls can only be truly nourished through the grace and life of Jesus. He longs to fill us with all that we need to live joyful and peaceful lives in him. Let us always be open to the spiritual food that the Lord offers in word and sacrament. Let us always be aware of the importance of having well-fed souls in Jesus.

(Acts 8:26-40)

"He replied, 'How can I, unless someone instructs me?'"

The Holy Spirit prompted St. Philip to travel to a certain area where he came upon an Ethiopian who was studying Scripture. The man asked for St. Philip's help in understanding, and all in his household came to believe and were baptized. It is important for us to learn from the Ethiopian, who was not afraid to say that he did not understand but was open to learning all that he could about God's Word in Scripture. Like the Ethiopian, we are called to seek instruction so that we can learn and have our faith strengthened in the power of God's Word. We are called to seek out knowledge of Jesus so that we can more easily persevere in our calling as Christians. In learning we gain strength and courage so that we are able to better handle hardship and sorrow. Learning of the majesty and goodness of our God grounds us so that we cannot be blown away by any wind of temptation or deceit that comes our way. There is much in this world to tempt us and lead us away from the Lord. It is in learning and knowledge that we remain strong and focused, solidly grounded in our faith.

Were Not Our Hearts Burning!

(Jeremiah 17:5-8)

"Thus says the Lord: cursed is the man who trusts in human beings, who seeks his strength in flesh, whose heart turns away from the Lord."

All of us know that human beings are weak. Each of us as a human being has faults. Not one of us is perfect. Only God is perfect. Jeremiah reminds us that when we put our trust in human beings, we can often times be disappointed. Jeremiah tells us that we must put our trust in God. We will never be disappointed when our faith and trust is placed in the Lord. We have all experienced the hurt of being disappointed in someone who should have been trustworthy. Even in our churches we can see the effects when people who should be trustworthy disappoint us. We are all aware of people who have left the Lord because they were let down by someone who betrayed their trust. Let us pray for the grace to trust God with all of our hearts. Let us pray that we always be aware of the trustworthiness of our most gracious and merciful God. Let us pray for forgiveness and mercy for ourselves when in our weakness we let others down, and for all who have let us down in our lives.

17

HE WILL COME AGAIN IN GLORY

We have been created for something much better than we have in this life. In his great love for us, God, our Father, sent his Son to redeem us, to open the gates of heaven that through him we might have everlasting life. It is God's plan that everything in heaven, on earth, and under the earth be subject to his Son, Jesus Christ. He is our King. He has promised to come again in glory, when he will judge the living and the dead. We live in the hope of that promise. We await that day with joy, for we will be united with all of redeemed creation as a living sacrifice to God, our heavenly Father, through his Son, Jesus, in the power of the Holy Spirit.

PRAYER

Jesus our King, help us to understand that this life on earth is but a speck of time compared to the eternal life to which you call us. Strengthen our faith and hope in you, our most majestic King. Help us to live this life with boldness and courage with our eyes always directed to the life to come, where every tear will be wiped away and we will reign with you in joy forever.

Were Not Our Hearts Burning!

(John 16:16-20)

"So they said, 'What is this "little while" [of which he speaks]? We do not know what he means.'"

Jesus explains to the apostles that he must leave them, but also says that he is going to prepare a place for them. He knows that they will miss him, but tells them that they will soon see him in all of his glory and majesty in heaven. Jesus reminds us of that very same thing. Like the apostles, we do not fully understand what the Lord means by a "little while." In fact, none of us knows when the Lord will come for us, but we know that he will come, and we know that we must always be prepared. We must be prepared for the Lord to come at any minute. We will always be ready if we lead good and holy lives every day. Jesus reminds us that although it may seem like a long time to us, it is truly just a little while compared to the eternity we will spend with him in heaven. Let us always remain close to the Lord, living in his light and love, so that the day he comes for us we will be ready to accompany him to heaven where we will live in joy for all eternity.

He Will Come Again In Glory

(Acts 17:22-34)

"God has overlooked the time of ignorance, but now he demands
that all people everywhere repent because he has established a day
on which he will judge the world with justice, through a man he has
appointed, and he has provided confirmation for all by raising him
from the dead."

We live in the time of God's mercy. His mercy gives us strength and hope.
His mercy builds up our faith. St. Paul reminds us, however, that the day
of his judgment is coming. Each of us will be judged according to our
deeds and the way in which we live our lives. St. Paul tells us that when
judgment day comes for us there will be no excuses. He reminds us that
God has given us every grace and blessing so that we can successfully
live good and holy lives on this earth. He continues to shower his grace
and mercy on us, and has given us the gift of the Holy Spirit to teach
and guide us. We already share in the victory of Jesus, who died and
rose again, and who now sits at the right hand of God where he makes
intercession for us with the Father. Let us live each day to the fullest in
the light and truth, reminding ourselves that only God knows the day
of judgment. Let us live confident lives in the Lord, knowing that he
continues to pour his grace and mercy upon us, providing everything
that we require to live lives of courage and holiness.

Were Not Our Hearts Burning!

(Luke 21:5-11)

"When you hear of war and insurrections, do not be terrified; for such things must happen first, but it will not immediately be the end."

We know that one day the world will end. One day Jesus will come again in glory to judge the living and the dead. In this passage we read that the people of Jesus' time were just as anxious about when this would occur as are many in our world today. There are many different cults and religious factions that base their entire belief system on knowing when the end will come. We have seen the disastrous results when these predictions do not come true. The world will end in God's time. Jesus also tells us this is something that need not concern us too much if we follow his teachings and commandments every day. We are called to live every day as if it were our last day. He tells us that if we live in his light, striving for holiness, the matter of when the final day comes will not be something that causes apprehension or fear in our lives. Jesus calls us to live confidently in him, knowing that when we live by his Word and in his light, we need never be frightened, nor will we ever come to harm. He promises that if we stay close to him, when the end does come he will call us to live with him in the presence of the Father, forever.

To order additional copies of

WERE NOT OUR
HEARTS BURNING!

Have your credit card ready and call:

1-877-421-READ (7323)

or please visit our web site at
www.pleasantword.com

Also available at:
www.amazon.com
and
www.barnesandnoble.com

Printed in the United States
43026LVS00004B/109-510

9 781414 105154